INDIAN FICTION IN ENGLISH

INDIAN FICTION IN ENGLISH

Edited by
PRAMOD KUMAR SINGH

ATLANTIC PUBLISHERS AND DISTRIBUTORS

Published by
ATLANTIC PUBLISHERS AND DISTRIBUTORS
B-2, Vishal Enclave, Opp. Rajouri Garden, New Delhi-27
Phones : 5413460, 5429987

Sales Office
4215/1, Ansari Road, Darya Ganj, New Delhi-110 002
Phones : 3273880, 3285873, 3280451
Fax : 91-11-3285873
e-mail : info@atlantibooks.com
web : www.atlanticbooks.com

ISBN 81-7156-945-5

Typeset at
APD Computer Graphics, Delhi

Printed in India at
Nice Printing Press, Delhi

PREFACE

Indian English Literature has earned widespread reputation both in India and abroad. It has come to have a significant place in the world's literature. The Indo-English novelists are now recognised among the greatest novelists of the world and winning international prizes and awards. The credit goes to the trio : Raja Rao, Mulk Raj Anand and R.K. Narayan, who earned international recognition for Indo-English fiction. The novelists of the later phase such as : Manohar Malgoankar, Nayantara Sahgal, Arun Joshi, Chaman Nahal, Bhabani Bhattacharya, Anita Desai, Khushwant Singh, B. Rajan and others have helped in shaping the modern Indian Novel in English. The novelist of latest phase such as : Salman Rushdie, Arundhati Roy, Amitav Ghosh, Vikram Chandra, Vikram Seth, Rohinton Mistry, Raj Kamal Jha and others have made the Indian Novels in English as the best selling novels of the world. The Indian English novels have been translated almost into all the languages of the world on account of its immense popularity all over the countries.

Fiction, being the most powerful form of the literary expression today, has achieved a prestigious position in the Indo-English literature. The novel, although born very recently, has acquired a place as a distinct literary form very rapidly. The Indian novels mirror the microcosmic India caught in the crucible of traditions, conventions and social changes. Its characters are the replica of common Indians. A critical response to the Indo-English fiction, thus, will be a true representation and a total response to the Indo-English Literature.

I am grateful to the contributors for their scholarly papers. I am deeply beholden to my brothers Anand Prakash Singh and

Rajendra Prasad Singh, Advocate, for their incessant encouragements. I am grateful to my colleagues Prof. R.K. Sinha and Prof. K.K. Singh for their assistance. I am thankful to my wife Sanju, son Harsh and daughter Tanya who freed me from other domestic engagements when the manuscript was being compiled. I express my thankfulness to M/s Atlantic Publishers and Distributors, New Delhi who gladly accepted to publish it.

Pramod Kumar Singh

CONTENTS

CONTRIBUTORS LIST

Ramesh Kumar Srivastava is Professor and Head, Department of English, Guru Nanak Dev University, Amritsar.

Prabhat Kumar Pandeya is a Professor in English at Banaras Hindu University, Varanasi.

R.N. Rai is a Professor in English, Banaras Hindu University, Varanasi.

V.K. Arora is a Reader at Government Autonomous College, Ajmer (Rajasthan).

Jagdish Prasad Singh is Reader in English at S.N. College, Kaira Deo (Bihar).

Siyaram Prasad Sinha is an I.A.S. Officer in Bihar Cadre.

Mrs. Roma Singh is a Research Scholar at V.K.S. University, Ara (Bihar).

Rajesh Kumar Sinha is a senior lecturer at S.P. Jain College, Sasaram (Bihar).

Krishna Kant Singh is a lecturer at S.P. Jain College, Sasaram (Bihar).

R.K. Gupta is a Research Scholar at J.P. University, Chapra (Bihar).

G. Rai is Professor and Head, Department of English, D.D.U. Gorakhpur University, Gorakhpur (U.P.).

Ashok Singh Rao is a lecturer in English at M.K. Saboo P.G. College, Pilani (Rajasthan).

Ramesh Kumar Gupta is a research-scholar in J.P. University, Chapra.

Shayam S. Agarwalla is a Principal, Dr. Ram Manohar Lohia College, Ranchi.

P.K. Singh is a lecturer in English, S.P. Jain College Sasaram.

K.K. Singh is a lecturer in English, S.P. Jain College Sasaram.

Pradipsinh B. Rathod is a lecturer in English, G.D. Modi College of Arts, Palanpur (Gujarat).

1

Khushwant Singh's *The Company of Women* : A Fictional Fantasy of Sizzling Sex

PRAMOD KUMAR SINGH

Khushwant Singh, born on February 2, 1915 at Hadali in West Punjab, is one of the most distinguished writers of India. He is author of four novels : *Train to Pakistan* (1956), *I Shall Not Hear the Nightingale* (1956), *Delhi* (1990) and *The Company of Women* (1999). He was awarded the Punjab Government Prize for being a 'Distinguished men of letters in India' in 1970 and 'Padma Bhusan' in 1974. His book on history of Sikhs has earned "Nishan-e-Khalsa Award" for him and doctorate from Guru Nanak Dev University.

Singh's latest novel *The Company of Women* may be regarded as "the millennium's last Great Indian Lascivious Novel giving the voyeuristic view of male and female anatomy and titillating accounts of the innumerable sexual encounters of his protagonist."[1] The author's narrative skill is so superb that a reader feel like watching a blue film rather than reading a fictional novel. Some critics say that the novel is neither erotic, nor funny, but it is in fact a sad novel. The noted novelist Shobha De, like other critics, condemns the novel for its peculiar theme and says, "I may write something far stronger in future. And no, I'll definitely not write *The Company of Women*; it gives sex a bad name. My fantasies happens to be more imaginative. Khushwant should never have written the book. It was like a SAARC conference on Bedding your neighbours. It also exposed him as India's most non-erotic writer and reconfirmed what a few have always believed, sex, in Khuswant's case, has always been in his head."[2]

The novel begins with its hero Mohan Kumar, a successful Delhi's businessman, breaking off with his wife, and his everlasting "Lusty" efforts to set up a more flexible arrangement for appeasement of his physical needs. The initial endeavour begins at his home with the sweepress and extends to the wide world of lonely women beyond the neighbourhood to the Princeton, having most bizarre of his "triumph" in one night encounter with a devout Muslim woman from Pakistan. The novel chronologically presents the most sensous pictures of the nine women with whom, the hero beds, including his wife. Of the eight on the description, one each is African, American, Kashmiri Pundit, Muslim, Dalit Hindu, Hindu Brahmin, Tamilian Christian, Goan Roman Catholic, Sri Lankan Buddhist and an unnamed women of easy virtue in Bombay. Singh seems to have extending the slogan that the love and sex know no caste, class and community bar. He further confirms his belief that lust is more important than love : Love cannot last very long without lust. Lust has no time-limit and is the true foundation of love and affection.

Living engaged in several sexual encounters, Mohan Kumar does not see anything wrong in adultery as it has some advantages also. He thinks that in fact adultery "did not destroy a marriage; quite often it proved to be a cementing factor, as in cases where the husband could not give his wife as much sex as she needed, or where the wife was frigid. It was silly to condemn adultery as sinful; it often saved marriages from collapsing. It could have saved his.'' (p. 8)

After the enraged wife of Mohan, Sonu, left home, he becomes impatient for fulfilment of sexual needs and his unlimited and unrestricted sexual appetite overpowers him. He starts eyeing at his sweepress, Dhanno, who looked him "full-bosomed" having a "narrow waist". He feels like agreeing with the version of his college mates who believed that sweeper women are the best lovers and are also "uninhibited, wild and hot". In a bid to win her favours, he gives her a hundred rupees note from his wallet and spoke some sympathetic words. Dhanno, who was herself waiting for such opportunity, shows her positive response quickly. One day when she was cleaning his bedroom, Mohan bolted the door from the inside and "kissed her on her lips and fondled her breasts. She responded vigorously. He slipped his hand inside her kameez to fell her breasts. They were firmer than his wife's and the nipples were much harder. Dhanno slipped her shirt off over her shoulders and coyly looked down at her feet. Mohan undid the cord of her salwar and let it fell to the floor. Dhanno was stark naked" (p. 23). She came a lot quicker than him but soon collapsed with a long gurgle like an animal being slaughtered. Mohan felt triumphant and proud of his manliness.

But he could not remain satisfied by the charity of his sweepress. He soon started looking for another opportunity of encounter. He gave an advertisement in the newspaper inviting applications from the sensuous lonely women. He gets the first response from a Brahmin lonely women Mrs. Sarojini Bhardwaj, a doctorate in English literature, teaching undergraduates in a college at Rewari. She was an unfulfilled soul living separated from his husband since long time. She came to Mohan's house and started living there being introduced as a distant relative. At night, both took a little drink to warm up their moods. The Mohan "undid the belt of her gown and cupped one of her breasts in his hands. Indeed, she was not as well endowed as his wife or Dhanno or any of the other he had bedded. The difference made her more desirable. He kissed her nipples and took one breast in his mouth. She began to gurgle with pleasure. 'Don't neglect the other one', she murmured. He did the same to the other breast. He unbuttoned his trousers and she felt his stiff penis throb against her belly. 'My God you are big', she exclaimed in alarm! 'This thing will tear me to pieces'. She clasped it between her thighs to prevent it piercing her. 'Promise you won't hurt me. Remember I'm very small and have had no sex for a very, very long time" (pp. 47-48). Mohan felt much elated, powerfully macho and grandly overpowering. But soon Mohan was compelled to bid farewell to Mrs. Sarojini due to growing resentment along the servants and gossips among other acquaintances. Before being separated from each other, they undergo a final encounter in a different style. Mohan "sat down in his chair, legs apart, exposing himself to her. She undid her dressing gown and came over and sat astride him. She put her hands on his shoulder and leaned back, so they could both see and marvel at how a small opening like hers could swallow up his huge organ. All of it, down to its hairy roots.

They made love not in the privacy of their bedrooms but in the moonlit balcony" (p. 59). Thereafter, both got into a tight embrace and separated from each other.

Mohan recollects his sexual encounter with her senior Ms. Jessica Browne, a tall, slender and chocolate-brown American girl, during his college days in Princeton. He got easily mix up with her as Americans to him, are very easy to get on with and are very open, frank and aggressively friendly. She used to teach him tennis and as such the tennis court was their regular dating point. One day when Mohan appreciated her beauty, she all of sudden slipped off her blouse and skirt. She was certainly beautiful in the African way, jet black fuzzy hairs, lustrous eyes and protruding breasts with large black nipples. Jessica thereafter took him on her bed and pulled him on her. Mohan "had never imagined sex could be so thrilling" and so he wished it to last longer. Both made love four times before they dropped off.

Yasmeen, a muslim student from Pakistan, was her next meeting at the Princeton during college days. They met at lecture hall when Dr. Ashby was delivering a lecture on religion. Mohan was hurt at her absurd questions relating Hinduism. She asked as to why Hindu worship a monkey or an elephant as a god. Initially they undergo into an argument but soon they became friendly. One day she took him by his hand and let him to her bedroom. ''She took off everything except her jewellery. Her skin was soft but flabby. Her big breasts sagged and she have shaved her pubic hair" (p. 100). None of the girl Mohan had bedded shaved their privates. He was "surprised to see that a woman so large, who had borne two children, had such a small vagina" (p. 100). Mohan says, "while I gazed at her figure, she took off my shirt and pulled down my trousers. She gasped at what she saw. 'Mashallah' what have you got there? Do all Hindus have organ of this size? It must be their reward for worshipping the phallus! She fondled it for a while with her pudgy hands, her lips glued to mine. She pulled me over her and stretched her thighs wide to receive me. I entered her. She moaned with pleasure and locked her legs behind my back. She ate up my face with bites and passionate kisses. We came together" (p. 109). Both became soon exhausted and went into the bathroom for wash.

After coming back from America, Mohan remain unbedded for a few weeks. He became soon restless as he had got used to bedding women almost on a daily basis and sometimes two in one day. He was soon married to Sonu who was the daughter of a rich businessman Rai Bahadur Lala Achint Ram. The matrimonial started in very cordial atmosphere. Mohan and her wife, Sonu, went Shivaliks for a money-moon. In a very cozy atmosphere, they started loving and fonding each other. He explains his foreplay; "I persisted in kissing her again and again, all over her face and back to her lips. She began to respond to my overtures. I slipped my hand beneath her blouse. For a moment she went stiff, then let me fondle her. I felt her breasts getting warmer under my palm and her nipples hardened like cherry stones. I wasn't sure if it was the night time to take her" (p. 155). He further says, "I could not hold myself any longer and lunged into her. She let out a loud scream of paid and slapped the sides of the bed like a live butterfly flapping its wings when a pin is stuck into it. After months of celibacy, I had a tankful of semen stored up. I pumped it into her. She continued to whimper for some time. 'You brute', she said, 'see what a mess you have made of me. She switched on the table lamp. The white bed-sheet was splattered with blood. Semen oozed out of her' (p. 159). They came back to home due to sudden illness of Sonu in the midway of honeymoon.

After sometime, Sonu becomes pregnant. Mohan thinks that the present house may be shorter for the family now. He decides to purchase a big house and to give a big surprise to Sonu and a gift for his new born son. He purchases the new house and name it after his son — 'Ranjit Villa'. Sonu comes back to the home with the new born son. Two nurses also come to look after the child. The two nurses were respectively Mary Joseph, a Roman Catholic from Tamil Nadu and Ittirra Mathew, Syrian Christian from Kottayam in Kerala. Long precautionary separation with Sonu keeps him thirsty and so sexual instinct starts perturbing him. One night Mathew Joseph comes to say him goodnight and stirs his sleeping 'Shaitan'. Mohan explains what happens then, "Marry Joseph came to say goodnight to me. I don't know what came over me. I took her in my arms and kissed her passionately. She did not resist. 'Saar, somebody may come in. It is not safe'. I bolted my study room from the insides and pushed her on my bed. She was quite willing. She pulled up her white shirt and took off her panties. I tore open her blouse and went hungrily for her large breasts. She stretched her thighs wide apart. As I entered her exclaimed, 'Aiy Aiy Yo! Saar, you are very big. I like it very much; she responded vigorously to my thrusts. We climaxed together." He further says, "And every night she thrusts her hips up at me, matching my desperate rhythm, leaving me in no doubt that she liked it very much" (pp. 176-77). Sonu soon senses that something is wrong. Her sixth sense warns that her security is being threatened and something wrong is going on under the roof. About a fortnight later, she announced the departure of nurses and so the game is over.

The matrimonial relation between Sonu and Mohan gradually becomes bitter. Mohan's father leaves home and goes to settle at an Ashram in Haridwar as Sonu dislikes his presence in the house. Mohan is hurt and drops his father at Haridwar unwillingly for the sake of peace in the house. The little Ranjit crys for his grandfather and hits the aya with his fists finding his 'Dada' nowhere in the house. Sonu gives birth to another child and their matrimonial life somehow pulls on. Mohan's father dies all of sudden at Haridwar and he gets information some days after the death. So he could not have even the last glimpse of his beloved father. He goes to Haridwar for immersion of his father's ashes. After coming back from Haridwar, he becomes reluctant to put up with the spree of nagging of her wife. In fact, Mohan's father was a binding force between the two. The idea of separation often coming in the mind of Mohan, was suppressed by him, as it was not to be approved by his religious and cultured father. He was of opinion, like any traditional Hindu father, that relation between husband and wife is for whole 'Janma'.

One day some disputes starts between them on a flimsy reason. Mohan lost his cool and slaps her. She too bursts into ire and crys at him trembling with rage and humiliation. She leaves the home for ever along with her both children. Mohan becomes lonely and disoriented after departure of his wife and children. One evening when he returns from office, he finds couple of policemen and Dhanno in their custody. The sub-Inspector informs that a complaint was lodged in the police station about the theft in two houses where Dhanno was employed. Many stolen properties were recovered by the police on raid and search of her quarter. The Sub-inspector asks

Mohan to identify the goods stolen from his house but he refuses as a gesture of favour to her for sharing the bed with him.

Mohan thereafter scrutinize the letters and invites Molly Gomes of Goa. She comes Delhi and stays at his residence. At night, both come in full mood and gets engaged in a physical encounter. Mohan explains, "Molly got up from her armchair and came over to me, without another word she slipped her blouse over her head and undid her bra. Two beautiful rounded breasts with black nipples emerged. She rested her arms on my shoulders and put up her mouth. I glued my lips to hers fondled her breasts with my warm hands. She unbuckled her skirt and let it drop the ground, then undid my belt, pulled down my trousers and felt my penis. Like the other women her first reaction was awe and wonder. ''Man, I've never seen anything of this size before. And believe me I've seen quite a few." He further says, "Only the twitching and milking of my organ assured me she was wide awake. It was blissful, it was prolonged. We took turns being on top of each other. We went on for an hour before I rolled over, bringing her under me and asked, 'Are you ready'" ? (pp. 221-22)

Khushwant is deeply aware of various social evils, oddities and eccentricities of society. He ironically highlights as to how many minor girls are being sexually exploited by their near relatives against sound social norms. Molly expresses as to how she was sexually abused by her uncle, who was nearly twenty years older than her. She expresses her anguish; "It was my own uncle, my mother's younger brother, a good twenty years older than me. Beast! 'Took advantage of poor, innocent me'. She laughed as she said this, but it was a mirthless laugh. Anyway, it happen one afternoon when he came to call on my parents and they were not at home. I was still in my school uniform short frock which ended above my knees, barely covering my thighs. He kissed me, as he always did, but this time on my lips. He sat down on the sofa, pulled me onto his lap and started kissing the back of my neck and my ears. I could feel his prick getting stiff and larger against my burn. He began to fondle my breasts, then squeeze them roughly. He was all out of breath. I knew he was up to no good and should have stopped him. But I was pretty worked up too by now and let him go on. He put the Sofa, pushed my frock up and pulled my panties down roughly. Then he fumbled with his trouser buttons, managed to get his fat dick out and shoved it in me, all in one go. He was an impatient man. It hurt and I screamed in agony. He pulled out after a violent thrusts and split all his gooey stuff on my thighs." (pp. 229-30)

Mohan thereafter meets Susanthika and their meeting soon blazed into romance. She was working with the High Commission of Sri Lanka. She comes closer to him for her interest in Hinduism. She was a Buddhist. Mohan tells about his romance with Susanthika; "I put my hand inside her bra. It was very tight. The buttons at the back snapped and her breasts were freed of their confines. I took her small, firm breasts in my mouth, first one, then the other. She put her head back, shut her eyes and 'aahd' and 'oohd' with pleasure as she kept ruffling my hairs with her fingers. She felt my member rise and throb under her. She stood up and tapped it with her bony hand. 'He's impatient for action. Came, she took my hand and led me to her bed. She lay down on her back and pulled her sari up above the waist. She wore no panties. She had planned it all. I was surprised to see how big her cunt was. She had obviously had plenty of sex. As I mounted her, she expressed no surprised about the size of my penis as most of the other woman had; she simply guided it in with her fingers and said, 'I feel like Ashoka's pillars entering me. I like it. Put in all you have." He further exclaims, "then for God's sake don't come inside me. I can't risk a pregnancy. I know it won't be much fun for you, but this, time, for my sake. She climaxed with her teeth dug into my neck and her hands clutching my hair. I pulled out just in time and squirted my semen on her thighs." (p. 265)

Mohan was surprised to know that Susanthika too, like Molly, was sexually abused by her near relative. She was exploited by her uncle (father's brother) at the age of sixteen. Susantha narrates, "I was sixteen. Nothing romantic about the deflowering. My own uncle, my father's younger brother. The usual thing, you know, a close relative whom you trust. It seemed harmless enough at first-kissing and cudding, that sort of thing. Then he thought he'd got me worked up and started playing with my breasts and stroking my crotch. I got frantic and before I know it he had me under him on the floor and tore into me" (p. 266). Thus, Mohan is amazed to know as to "how many girls are initiated into sex by their older relations or their parents' friends". (p. 267)

Mohan's last physical contact happens with an unknown lady of about thirty in Bombay. She decline to disclose her name despite Mohan's request. The encounter proves fatal for him. The lady was suffering from deadly disease AIDS. She lightly warns Mohan to use condom before sex but don't insist on his refusal. She was a call-girl who took thousand rupees before sharing him the bed. Mohan explains his physical encounter with her; "she obeyed; the blouse and the skirt came off first, then the bra and the panties. Mohan's member stiffened. He was delighted. In that one instant all the anxiety and frustration of the past several months was wiped out. He was his old self again. He pulled down his pants and showed her what he had" (p. 281). He further explains, "There was no passion in her movements. When he tried to kiss her on the lips, she turned her face away. She let him kiss and suck breasts. But her nipples did not harden. He went into her. She tried quick heavens to get him to come fast. He took his own good time, he had not had sex for months. When he came, she feigned a climax. It was all very mechanical but he was satisfied, relieved that he had not become impotent".[3] (p. 281)

Mohan invites many lonely girls to come and have sex with him. This is not an isolated case or mere fictional imagination of Khushwant Singh. In fact this is in reality happening in different parts of our country especially in metropolitan cities. The people from elite or higher middle class now frequently inviting male or female to come for physical changes. Such invitation are being made through a special 'ad' column of many sex magazines such as 'Fantasy', 'Bombayite', 'Debonair' etc. Khushwant Singh ironically satirizes this truth through his present novel. Such cultural degradation causing AIDS in Urban and Metropolitan cities is Khushwant's main concern of the novel. Social evils such as extra-marital relation, incestuous sex, sexual exploitation of dalits and minors, etc., are the real heroes of the novel.

After nearly six months of the last sexual encounter with the unnamed women at Bombay, Mohan suffers from illness and his health began to deteriorate. Earlier he had never fallen into illness. He began to lose weight rapidly and some medicines taken could hardly provide him any relief. Her office's assistant Vimla Sharma takes care of him. She calls a doctor, Dr. Malhotra, for check up and treatment. After check up — reports were examined by him. Dr. Malhotra asks him about his sexual activities. Dr. Malhotra asks, "Did you use condoms all the time" (p. 289). Mohan replies in negative to his utter consternation and dismay. Doctors informs that he is now HIV positive. Mohan becomes sad and gloomy. The novel ends with attempted suicide of Mohan by taking thirty sleeping pills at a time.

Some critics call the novel a 'fine fictional art'. Some others say 'that the novel is neither erotic nor funny, but it is, ultimately, a sad book'.[4] Kumar moves through a series of bed partners neither discovering anything for himself nor offering to the readers any notable insight, experience or realisation. There is indeed a tragic moment at the end of the novel when, looking at his limp "Baby python", he showers the worst invectives on it for getting him into his deadly predicament. Just at the moment "he was reminded of all the pleasure he had known in life, and knew little that he only had this little snake to thank for all of it". Khushwant indeed ironically campaign against the 'deadly disease', when shows Kumar getting AIDS, all in a matter of just six months from unprotected sexual encounter in Mumbai and ultimately dies. Throughout the novel, he neither defies social norms, nor pays a moral price for his philandering.

NOTES

1. Hason Surror, *The Hindu,* September 19, 1999.
2. Sobha De, *Hindustan Times*, November 21, 1999.
3. Khushwant Singh, *The Company of Women,* (Viking Penguin Book India (P) Ltd., New Delhi, 1999).
4. M. Paranjape, *Khushwant Singh's One-Night Stand; The Indian Express*, September 19, 1999.

2

Clinton-Helen-Bashiam Relationship in Markandaya's *The Coffer Dams*

RAMESH KUMAR SRIVASTAVA

In her novel *The Coffer Dams*, Kamala Markandaya gives the old husband-wife-lover triangle a political hue by involving in it an Englishman, an Englishwoman and an Indian tribesman. The time-tested formula in which a third person intrudes to disrupt husband-wife relationship would have appeared something tame and stale but for the fact that Markandaya has so painstakingly tailored everything to her ideological and fictional needs that its laboriously-striven perfection smacks more of the heavily-painted paper-flowers rather than of the natural ones. While Clinton-Helen relationship is characterised by mere form and without the least sustaining warmth, Helen's love for Bashiam originates from her sense of pity, of adventure, of savouring something raw and primitive but no less to spite her husband. In Manohar Malgoankar's *A bend in the Ganges*, Sundari has sex with Gian Talwar to spite her husband after ascertaining that the latter would watch it with a set of binoculars. Similarly, in Ramesh K. Srivastava's novel *Neema*, Jeewan's wife has sex with Rasik Lal to spite her impotent husband who had falsely charged her with having illicit relations with his younger brother. In *The Coffer Dams*, Helen's motive in having sex with Bashiam is not entirely to spite her husband Clinton as it is in the cases of Sundari and Neema but also to prove a Wordsworthian view that the tribesmen, by being in close proximity to nature, are more human, their conversation more natural and they therefore are more attractive than their urbanized counterparts.

Howard Clinton is essentially a war-savaged person who finds satisfaction in building structures rather than human relationships. His insistence on efficiency makes him work-conscious, mechanical and a creature of reason, while Helen is being of feelings and emotions. He delights in meticulously planning the construction work and in collecting statistics whereas Helen goes around the forests and tribesmen's settlements. His vision of the dam blinds him to the hapless peasantry to which Helen, his wife, is irresistibly drawn. Being half the age of her husband, Helen has a good power of communication which he lacks. He considers the tribesmen as "savages" and "sods" : she as human beings. She claims to have affinity with Indians in her earlier life; he denies it even in the present one.

Clinton's and Helen's widely-different temperaments make their relationship far from being harmonious more of the builder than a husband, he insists on order, efficiency and perfection at the cost of human relationships. His work and his wife fall into two separate compartments with the larger one for the former. Clinton's work-mania dehumanizes him so much that neither the rattling cottages, nor the deaths of forty people in blasts affect him. As opposed to Helen who is mobile and desirous of mixing with others, Clinton is reserved and attributes the absence of proper communication with the tribesmen to his advanced age which she repudiates.

Unlike Clinton whose skin breeds superiority complex within him and does not let him have a good relationship with the dark-skinned tribesmen, Helen visits numerous settlements along the river and gets on well with the tribesmen. Clinton usurps their site for the Englishmen's quarters by uprooting the tribesmen while Helen feels touched even by a few broken bits of pottery. Clinton's selfishness and inconsiderateness contrast with Helen's consideration and helpful attitude. Clinton's imposition of mass fines on the tribesmen is diametrically opposed to Helen's helping them with food to ward off starvation deaths. Her belief in the harmlessness of green snakes infuriates Clinton for whom it is symptomatic of her total faith in what the tribesmen tell.

Clinton is disciplined and conforms to the prevalent norms while Helen is a freak and rebel to the rule governing the memsahibs. His ideas move along a fixed track whether about the coffer dams, the

Englishmen or the tribesmen — and do not deflect easily. He coldly asks Helen, "Are you trying to teach me my business?" When she open-mindedly advises him to slow down the work on the construction of the dam. Clinton is a spokesman of civilization; Helen of nature, primitivism and simplicity of life. As a Christian, he scoffs at the tribesmen's worship of birds and animals whereas she is critical of Christianity which has made the people arrogant and desensitized. Unlike Clinton, she knows the value of the last rites of the dead tribesmen. Clinton has love for England and Englishmen whereas Helen is for India and Indians.

Since the novel is about the coffer dams, Clinton-Helen relationship occupies a secondary importance. However, its regression from marriage to mutual ignorance and suspicion, violence, infidelity and final reconciliation can be traced to five stages. In the first stage, their relationship begins with marriage after which Clinton comes to India for the construction of the dam and brings his wife along. By making them of widely different ages, Kamala Markandaya has already sown the seeds of incompatibility in marriage which are bound to bear fruits subsequently as does Anita Desai in making Gautam twice the age of Maya in *Cry, the Peacock.* Clinton's concern for the dam makes him neglect not only the "dreary saga of a hapless peasantry" (p. 9) but also Helen who sympathizes with the brown-colored tribesmen. Consequently, ignorance of each other's interests characterises their relationship in this stage. While Clinton goes for the single-minded pursuit of the dam, he fails to find why his wife does not need other Englishwomen's company and what keeps her preoccupied. Helen proclaims her love for him and allays his sprouting suspicion by denying involvement with anyone even when her interest lies in all sorts of people and things. Thus significantly large patches of ignorance characteries their relationship.

In the second stage, Clinton-Helen relationship develops serious cracks resulting in mutual indifference, neglect and suspicion. Clinton treats Helen on a level inferior to the inanimate dam, giving the impression that the two of them happen to be widely different people yoked together in marriage and characterised by mutual indifference. To her, Clinton's life appears hollow; that of the tribesmen wholesome. Markandaya seems to make Clinton's divided self compartmentalised — with machines at the worksite and with Helen at the bungalow, and who in his sleep dreams "sometimes of Helen and sometimes of the dam" (p. 31). At the worksite, Helen scarcely enters his thoughts but on his way back he anticipates meeting her. Significantly, when surrounded by the machines, he ill-treats the tribesmen. What keeps Helen humanized is that she shows no interest in the worksite, the machines, or even the non-human Clinton but visits settlements of the tribesmen. A few broken bits of pottery remind Helen and symbolise ruins of some woman's life with whom she identifies herself. Machines and human beings attract respectively Clinton and Helen. As Clinton does not remember his wife at the worksite," Helen fails to leave a note for her husband while wandering off into the jungle. Thus, far from being warm, ardent and passionate, which being recently married couple they were expected to be, they show mutual indifference, neglect and even suspicion. On Clinton's casual request to her to wear good cloths frequently, Helen complains of his indifference in not taking a note of her, and he confesses. "I ought to take more care of you. Lock you up, as wise men would" (p. 77).

Helen's growing concern for the tribesman makes Clinton suspicious and alarmed, particularly about her growing relationship with Bashiam, not yet sexual. The suspicion is something dark "without illumination, like a black sun : an intimation of danger" (p. 28) but on which he cannot precisely put a finger. The main reason of her attraction to the tribals is that she finds in them "natural springs of intercourse" which she cannot in Clinton and other Englishmen. Clinton is fragmented — mad after money and work, whereas amid fragile huts and poverty, she finds "whole people built whole lives" (p. 43). It is the absence of this wholeness in Clinton that sours their relationship.

The absence of a fully-satisfying relationship with Helen troubles Clinton. He finds Helen receding from him a little further each day as if slipping into someone's hands and therefore wishes to take possession of her, "carnally, spiritually, wholly' (p. 58). While Clinton talks of going back to England because India does not suit him, Helen blooms and looks "like a bride" (p. 65) as its climate and people agree with her.

In the third stage, Clinton recognises Bashiam as an adversary and his relationship with Helen approaches a breaking point. The incident of trapping birds gives a concrete shape to Clinton's suspicion of connection between Bashiam and Helen. Clinton who had always regarded Bashiam as a sod and jungliwallah, now in this stage recognises him as a man — "a ludicrous adversary" (p. 91) — someone who has to be reckoned with. On realisation that Helen has a soft corner for Das and Bashiam, Clinton grows wary of her references to any Indian, because he cannot reconcile to the Indian as an adversary.

The fourth stage comes in Helen's symbolic rejection of Clinton when she has sex with Bashiam. In order to exercise his control over his wife, Clinton rapes her and by doing so, severs the delicate thread of their relationship. When Helen wants the work on the dam to be slowed down in view of the deaths of labourers, Clinton decides to stick to the schedule. On her reminding his that the pace of construction was killing the labourers, Clinton not only inhumanly disregards them but accuses Helen of trying to teach him his business and that creates a visible tension between them.

In the fifth stage, the battleline between the two adversaries is drawn over the control of Helen. Clinton plans to physically damage Bashiam in order to reclaim his wife. It is the last ditch effort of Clinton to reassert the control of concrete and steel over human beings. His initial reluctance to take Bashiam's help in extricating the two trapped bodies arises out of the latter's failure to come to Clinton's terms. In getting the trapped bodies out, Clinton fails but Bashiam succeeds. Markandaya suggests that a mere fastidious, mechanized, even if intelligent person like Clinton is ineffective by being divorced from human beings whereas the primitive and uneducated people like Bashiam succeeds due to good equilibrium they have of the head and the heart. The disequilibrium in Clinton makes him like Hawthorne's Dr. Rappacini who sacrifice his daughter for a botanical experiment of human beings or like Roger Chillingworth in *The Scarlet Letter* who becomes inhuman in the pursuit of his cold-blooded revenge against the sensitive Arthur Dimmesdale.

Bashiam is the third angle of the triangle, and Helen-Bashiam relationship symbolises, to use A.V. Krishna Rao's words, "the forces of moderation and humane attitudes." On a closer scrutiny of the novel, it becomes obvious that Helen's relationship with Bashiam is not reciprocal on one-to-one basis. A certain degree of unnaturalness marks their relationship as if they were chess-board figures being moved by the novelist for some ideological purpose. If Clinton-Helen relationship lacks wholesomeness in the absence of the husband's human traits, Helen-Bashiam relationship lacks naturalness because of their widely different backgrounds. Clinton's relationship is based on the age-old institution of marriage whereas Bashiam, in his relationship with Helen, has neither any strong motivation, nor the tribal sanction.

Bashiam, an Indian tribesman, was born in the hills and adopted the traditional craft of woodcutting till the Englishmen uprooted him and his village in order to build the hydro-electric station. He is not a product of technical colleges but learns about electricity and machines from a discerning foreman in the course of his employment. In him the knowledge of the forest and the river is welded together with his training. His non-conformist nature makes him a stranger in the midst of the tribesmen. Clinton considers him a jungliwallah — "a primitive just come down off the trees" (pp. 23-24) to mean that his place was far below the Englishmen in the power scale.

Almost parallel to Clinton-Helen relationship which goes through five stages from marriage, mutual indifference, quarrel, severance of threads of love to reconciliation, Helen-Bashiam relationship, too, can be traced to five stages. In the first stage, it is confined to the level of curiosity. After coming to India, Helen finds a link-man and an interpreter in Bashiam. As the wife of Clinton, she commands respect from others, goes around in the forest, mixes with the tribesmen, meets Bashiam and is curious to know many things, particularly bird-trapping, in which the tribesman helps. Being kindhearted she is drawn to the victims and sufferers among the tribesmen. Thus the more Clinton harasses Bashiam and other tribesmen, the more she recedes from him and gravitates to them. Helen's opposition to Clinton's plan of shifting the tribesmen from their settlements and her concern over the bits of broken pottery show her growing rebellion against Clinton and her increasing attachment with the tribesmen and women with whom she identifies herself.

Contrary to Clinton's view who holds India responsible for most of his problems, the Indian climate suits Helen so much that she blooms and appears like a bride but which Millie suspects to be due to her relationship with Bashiam. Since Helen goes with an open mind and a sincere heart, she merges herself completely with the welcoming tribesmen-playing with their brown, pot-belied children, rubbing flea-powder into the dogs' yellow coats, watching men and women at work and marvelling that such a wholesome life could be found in these settlements as opposed to the fragmented lives of Englishmen, particularly that of Clinton.

If the first stage relates to the sprouting of Helen-Bashiam relationship on the level, of curiosity, the second stage marks its growth as a plant amidst the menacing weeds of rumours and scandals. It is here that Helen goes to see Bashiam in order to learn bird-trapping. Early in the morning, she feels cold and Bashiam spreads a shawl around her. In certain parts of the country, putting a shawl or a *chaddar* around a woman means making her one's wife. Even if Bashiam had done it to save her from cold, the symbolic significance can't be dismissed because the consummation between them does take place at a later stage.

The growth of Helen-Bashiam relationship leads to Clinton's recognition of Bashiam "as a man" (p. 91) and an adversary. This is significant progress from his being "sod", "tribesman" and "a faceless cog" in the first stage and who now is too important to be dismissed "as a ludicrous adversary" (p. 91). For Bashiam, the bird-trapping also amounts to Helen-trapping, as the bird is often used metaphorically for a member of the other sex. The growing relationship between Helen and Bashiam is reflected in her growing concern for Indians which makes Clinton jealous. She reproaches Clinton for perpetual blasting which rattles the tribesmen's cottages. The accidental deaths of both Englishmen and tribesmen make her suggest that the work on the dam be slowed down but Clinton's refusal pushes her further to the tribesmen's side. Clinton's act of raping her in order to assert his manhood severs the delicate threads of relationship between the husband and wife which makes her more towards Bashiam.

After the sexual act, Bashiam wished to go for work on the dam in the middle of the night, leaving Helen behind. To her, Bashiam's attitude of considering the dam more important than her appears no different from that of Clinton or Rawlings or Mackendrick. Because for Bashiam, too, the dam is "the central thing," the hub, round which "living and loving" revolve (pp. 137-38). Believing Bashiam to be more humanistic and closer to nature than Clinton could ever be, Helen had gravitated towards the tribesman but she shockingly discovers him to be different from Clinton only in degree, not in kind. Bashiam's detribalization, his duty-consciousness, and his punctuality in attending to his duties make him in some respects similar to Clinton. If Clinton had shown utter disregard to her feelings after raping her, Bashiam too disregards her by leaving her behind in order to go out to resume his work on the dam. In Bashiam's act of subordinating her to his work, Helen finds a shade of Clinton. Nevertheless, in totality, she finds Bashiam superior to Clinton.

Bashiam's readiness to do the work is from his conviction that the two trapped bodies belong to him and should not become impediments in the construction of the dam which is what they were proving to be. In spite of this consideration, he "wavered" and "would have withdrawn" but decides to do the work because he had taken Clinton's wife and felt that to him a debt was owed. This reasoning of Bashiam allows his humanistic image to suffer as if his obligation to Clinton for having slept with his wife overrode all other humanistic considerations. Though it was Helen who had gone to Bashiam, the sexual act was theirs, not his alone. In order to be free of this obligation, Bashiam decides to retrieve the bodies.

It is here that the fifth stage in Helen-Bashiam relationship is reached. Bashiam's refusal to share his thoughts and anxieties with Helen shows that the East is East and the West is West and only occasionally will they meet to part again. Not fully realizing that Clinton was trapping him with a faulty crane in revenge against the tribesman's relationship with Helen, Bashiam undertakes the work. His act of retrieving the two trapped bodies is symbolic of freeing humanity from stone-hearted people whereas Clinton's act of disallowing Mackendrick from warning Bashiam of the impending danger due to faulty crane means that a man in confrontation with nature on one hand and with non-human Clinton on the other may not be defeated but is bound to be damaged.

When badly wounded Bashiam drifts from coma to consciousness, Helen asks him, "Why did you do it?" and he replies, "There are somethings which one has to do" (p. 203). His act of holding on to the secret of his motive points out to the need of maintaining separate identities even after merging completely with Helen in the sexual act. There are regions "which must remain private to each" (p. 203). Helen realises that even after surrendering herself completely before him, she cannot claim the privilege of violating his privacy. On her question as to what Bashiam would do after the project is completed and they go back to England, he shows his self-respect by referring to many projects in the country as if to point out that neither Helen's nor her country's charm could budge him from India.

Markandaya's *The Coffer Dams* is a fervent plea but in vain for a romantic union of nature and primitivism with technological progress, now lost in the din of overriding materialistic considerations.

NOTES AND REFERENCES

1. Kamala Markandaya, *The Coffer Dams* (1969; Delhi : Hind Pocket Books, 1969), p. 124. Subsequent references to the book are from this edition and page numbers are given in parenthesis.
2. Elena J. Kalinnikova, *Indian-English Literature : A Perspective* (Ghaziabad : Vimal Prakashan, 1982), p. 162.
3. K. Madhavi Menon and A.V. Krishna Rao, "*The Coffer Dams* : A Critical Study," *Perspectives on Kamala Markandaya*, ed. by Madhusudan Prasad (Ghaziabad : Vimal Prakashan, 1984), p. 176.
4. A.V. Krishna Rao, "Continuity and Change in the novels of Kamala Markandaya," *Perspectives on Kamala Markandaya*, p. 16.
5. *Ibid*., p. 16.
6. K. Madhavi Menon and A.V. Krishna Rao, "*The Coffer Dams* : A Critical Study", p. 176.
7. Haydn Moore Williams, "Victims and Virgins : Some Characters in Markanday's Novels," *Perspectives on Kamala Markandaya*, p. 32.
8. K.R. Srinivasa Iyengar, *Indian Writing in English* (New Delhi : Sterling Publishers, 1984), p. 449.
9. A.V. Krishna Rao, "Continuity and Change in the Novels of Kamala Markandaya," p. 16.
10. K. Madhavi Menon and A.V. Krishna Rao, "*The Coffer Dams* : A Critical Study," p. 165.

3

In an Alien Country : Cross-cultural Experience in *Bye-Bye Blackbird*

PRABHAT KUMAR PANDEYA

Bye-Bye Blackbird by Anita Desai is an important novel on the subject of Asian immigrants, particularly the Indians, in England. In short, it is the story of an Indian couple, Adit Sen and his twenty-four-year old English wife Sarah, and Dev the newly arrived friend from India. In the beginning Adit is pretty comfortable in English society with a middle-rung white collar job, an amiable English wife, fully at home in the alien country : "I'm happy here. I like going in to the local for a pint on my way to Sarah. I like wearing good tweed on a foggy November day. I like the convent Garden opera house. I like the girls here I like their nylon stockings....I like thatched cottages and British history and the letters in *The Times,* Dev with his background of English literature is critical of everything English, even though his ulterior motive in coming to London is to find a job. Sarah, with all her understanding and cooperation, finds herself misfit in company of the Indians who gather periodically at someone's house. She and her white acquaintance Bella, married to another Indian, fail to appreciate Indian jokes that go round in such gatherings : "But Sarah and Bella sat in stiff silence, their Anglo-Saxon faces impassive. They had learnt exactly how much of this foreign world was theirs to tread and had given up their early attempts, made out of curiosity and a desire to join, to interpret jokes which seemed entirely to depend an such matters as a Bengali's accent or a Panjabi's eating habits or a Bihari's intellectual limitations of which they naturally had no experience or comprehension.... Sarah, who was only vaguely aware of the existence of such jokes, had her lips pressed together in a thin smile of boredom." (25) Dev is also critical of his compatriots. He bursts out at Adit : "You lazy immigrants. God you should go mad-mad, when even schoolboys can call you names on the streets, when you find that the London docks have three kinds of lavatories — Ladies, Gents, and Asiatics." (17)

But the irony of the novel is that Adit, the Indian with a comfortable job, family, English wife, fully at home in his adopted country, by the end of the novel decides to leave England for good to India with his English wife, and Dev, who has been critical of the English and England, decides to stay back in England, and to cap it, he steps into Adit's shoes, occupying his flat and replacing him in the job at a small tourist agency. Thus, in the novel all the three major characters Adit, Sarah, and Dev — have cross-cultural experience, but each of them reacts individually to the same situation. The novel also touches on racial problem and feeling in England. This feeling becomes sharper when it comes to a colonizer nation like England who has ruled over us for a long time. It is not simply white man's burden but also the feeling of superiority by virtue of their being ruler over us.

Sarah's position is peculiar, and at times pathetic. By marrying an Indian she had broken the tacit code of English society and, thus, falling in the eyes of the British. Her colleagues in the school are critical and satirical towards her. Consequently, she withdraws into her shell avoiding questions about her husband and future plans : "So she had to learn, through the years, to keep others talking of themselves rather than allow them to refer to her, and the tea-break was for her an exhausting, demanding and hair raising exercise in such tactics." (37) She suffers from a sense of inferiority because of her marrying an Indian, and for this she has to suffer the taunts from her colleague, Julia : "If she is that ashamed of having an Indian husband, why did she go and marry him?" (37) She fails to reconcile with Indian ethos. For example, why in Indian culture the cow should be holy and other pet animals repugnant. When Adit and Dev refuse to eat the rice sniffed at and, hence, polluted by her pet cat Bruce. Sarah was attached to pets and she does not think she could live in a house without pets somehow." And when she asks Adit, "But you have your sacred cows, Adit, right in your streets?" she is only snubbed and brow-beaten by her husband "That's quite different." Adit said sternly, "quite different." (50) In face of such irrational things the poor woman becomes confused and out of sorts and gives up in exasperation.

Sarah's cross-cultural experience lands her in trouble, a kind of schizophrenia. She didn't know who she was. She had to suffer the taunts of school children who took malicious delight in calling her "Hurry, Mrs. Curry ?" (38)

Her case, in cultural context, is really hopeless, although by the end of the novel she would be going to India with her husband. We are not told how she would adjust herself in the new milieu. What comes out clearly is the fact that she is a sincere woman trying to live honestly, whether in her own country or her would be adopted country, India. The two key-words are sincerity and truth. In spite of her incomprehension of Indian way of life she does realise that in spite of poverty, disease, hunger and over-population she is alive. She appreciates the closer knit society of India with more human touch. When Dev, fed up with reserve insulated life of London, bursts out, and for a change, speaks good of Calcutta life for its intimacy and contact Sarah likes it : "That must be nice," (56) for she knows her own country and people where "everyone is a stranger and lives in hiding. They live silently and invisibly. It would happen nowhere in India." (56) This brings to our mind "the lean solicitor" of *The Waste Land* where each is locked in his room. How typical of the English ?

For Dev visit to England is like an intellectual pilgrimage and so it is for any Indian who has the background of English literature. There is a peculiar feeling and thrill when one reaches the places one has read and taught in India, be it Dover beach or Westminster or the Thames. Dev notes "those elements that now serve to remind him he is not reading glaze-eyed Henry James or Galsworthy, but is walking inside the original of the scene he knows in description and pictures." (65) Adit and Dev both are brought up on English education and literature and no wonder that Wordsworth is quoted : "Adit and Dev, brought up as they were on dogeared copies of Palgraves's *Golden Treasury,* chant Earth has not any thing to show more fair :

Earth has not anything to show more fair :
Dull would be of soul who could pass by.... (67)

But Dev is equally critical of England and conscious of India's culture and as though to impress Adit and to display his knowledge of Sanskrit once while in a city bus passing through the Battersea power station he bursts forth in a Vedic hymn to Agni and to Adit's agony, Dev began to in tone shrilly, in Sanskrit :

Produce thy streams of flame like a broad onslaught, Go forth impetuous like a king with his elephant. Thou art and archer. Shoot thy sorcerers with thy hottest arrows, O Agni, send forth thy heat, thy winged flames.... (54)

But to Adit the trouble with Dev is "that you are too westernised." (69) Dev may take delight in reciting Vedic *richas* but he is not interested in visiting the Victoria and Albert Museum housing "The best collection of Moghul and Rajasthan miniatures." The very idea is dismissed as something ridiculous, "Don't be funny. Do you think I have come to London to see Indian paintings?" (60) He has come in search of greater things, a cultural and intellectual quest, as though he wanted to translate a vision : "He was determined to seek, discover and win the England of his dreams and reading, the England he had quickly seen was the most poetic, the most innocent and enduring of England, in a secret campaign. At the end, he believed he did." (168) But the fact remains that London, the city, can never be conquered : "Because London invited courtship, admiration, flirtation, enjoyment — but not conquest? Because London would not be conquered? Why? Willingly England had conquered his own country, then why — he sighed incoherently, feverishly — would she give nothing in return?'' (120) Earlier Dev presents a fantasy of Indian colonisation of England which is described as a harangue by the novelist but actually it is a wish-fulfilment fantasy on his part. In Petticoat Lane, seeing Indian goods and shopkeepers, Adit says, "It seems to me the East India Company come to take over England now." And this idea triggers Dev's fantasy.

Dev with 'his English Literature B.A. degree from Xavier College, Calcutta thinks himself as a cultural ambassador to England and wants to dispel the feeling that the Indians are in any way inferior to the British. He is at home in England. When he goes to the pub for the first time he is not at a loss : "Ye it was known, familiar, easy to touch, enjoy and accept because he was so well prepared to enter it — so well prepared by fifteen years of reading the books that had been his meat and drink, the English books that had formed at least one half of his conscious existence." (11) He wants to wash off the disgrace of colonial stamp of servility on the Indians. Because of his thorough grounding in English culture, language and literature he feels himself no worse than Englishman : "l am here...as an ambassador. I am showing these damn imperialists with their lost colonies complex that we are free people now, with our own personalities that this veneer of an English education has not obscured, and not afraid to match ours with theirs. I am here, he proselytised, to interpret my country to them, to conquer England as they once conquered India, to show them, to show them". (123) The fact is that Dev has a love-hate relationship with his ex-colonisers. But he finds excuse of for his gruffness towards the English, excuse for his vindictiveness. As pointed out by the novelist, he is hutting for British superciliousness, even if there is no such thing actually : "It is the beginning of Dev's obsessed search for signs of imperialist insolence in the bland manners of the British." (73) And that is why he is blunt towards Sarah's friend Christine Langford in Chapter 3.

But Adit knows better what had attracted Dev his old friend to this alien country, "this meeting of incongruous elements, of discordant natures and backgrounds?" He knew it will and so personally : "It was magic of England — her grace, her peace, her abundance, and the embroidery of her history and traditions — and the susceptibility of the Indian mind to these elements, trained and prepared as it was since its school days to receive, to understand and appreciate these very qualities. It was because of...East India Company and the missionaries who bore the Biblo and Palgrave's *Golden Treasury* under one arm and a bottle of whisky under the other, that Dev was padding contentedly about this enclosed garden in Hempshire and Adit...was smiling at the reconciliation of two cultures hovering in the air like a thrust with a laurel leaf held in its beak." (157) But in spite of all fire and brimstone Dev, by the end of the novel, is tamed to be one of the many Indian immigrants who make England their home. All his intellectual threadbaring, criticism, attack on the British and Britain peters out. Instead of he leaving England, it is Adit who goes away for good. As though England were a mohini, a siren who keeps netting Indians, or for that matter other aliens. To quote the novelist : "Somewhere, at some point that summer, England's green and gold fingers had let go of Adit and clutched at Dev instead. England had let Adit drop and fall away as if she had done with him or realised that he had done with her, and caught and enmeshed his friend Dev. It was as though there were an arbitrary act of England's, an abstract law to which Adit and Dev had quite unwittingly succumbed." (228-29) And this gives subtle suggestion that the hero of the novel is not a person, but a country that is England.

Adit's cross-cultural experience completes the full circle. He had come to England with high hopes. And from a distance England seems El Dorado. He struggles, picks up petty jobs, lives a tolerable life; first in provincial towns and then finally finds a place under the sun, the British sun. In Dev's words he sits pretty and he accepts it. With his English wife and a middle-rung job he is happy and contented. He has friends, social circle, house, job, and family and he has no hesitation to say that he loves England : "I like the pubs. I like the freedom a man has here : Economic freedom; I like reading posters in the tube.... And I like the Thames.... I like the feeling I can nip across the Channel for a holiday in Paris.... I like these fat old London women with faces like buns full of currants.... I like a weekend at the seaside. I even like the BBC." (18-19) He also accepts that he is a romantic, and hot a cynic like Dev : "I'm a romantic an old fashioned romantic and I don't feel ashamed of it — not here on the steps of St. Paul's with all the bells ringing." (69) Dev's bitterness is caused by his unemployment also, but Adit is sitting pretty : "yes, I'm sitting pretty," said Adit.... "I am very content as I am, but I know I'll be Director one day. My employers are very pleased with me—they see it, recognise drive and flair and imagination when they see it, you know." (104-5) Unlike his cynical, fault-finding friend, Adit loves his adopted country : "I love England. I admire England. I can appreciate her history and her poetry as much as any Englishman. I feel a thrill about Nelson's battle, about Waterloo, about Churchill." (164) From time to time he tries to improve upon Dev's bitter attitude towards England. Once he hits at his double standard, *i.e.*, his love for English poets and his disdain for the English and their country : "You Bengali, you, you know nothing and feel nothing for England. That's been clear to me ever since you arrived. Now you suddenly put on this long-haired, bird-feeling country poet act. What a fraud." (155) Adit is right, for "he was the connoisseur of English literature, of English history, not Dev, the sarcastic iconoclast" (155) and it is fraud, rather his realisation of fraud, that makes Adit decide to leave England for good. Even though apparently well adjusted in England with his cosy little world, Adit at times feels the artificiality of his existence in England.

Adit realised that the small India in England with his Indian friends, Indian food and music won't do. The places, pubs, streets that were so familiar to him became strange to him because of "the black sensation of not belonging." (181) The feelings that he had once hated in his compatriots — "the eternal immigrants who can never accept their new home and continue to walk the streets like strangers in enemy territory, frozen, listless" — engulf himself. Adit attributed this difficulty to belong to a foreign country to a lack of education and a sense of international citizenship. But he, of a sudden, himself became a victim : "But now his own education, his 'feel' for British history and poetry, fell away from him like a coat that has been secretly undermined by moths so that its sinews and tendons are gone and, upon being touched, crumbles quitely to dust upon the wearer's shoulders. Unclothed, Adit began to shiver in the cold...." (182) He himself couldn't explain his feelings : "It was not the occasional slights and insults directed against him as a stranger, a non-believer, that had finally proved too much for him, but the placidity, the munificence and the ease of England." (184) The things that he used to enjoy became "falsehood, the fallacy, the unnatural strain" (187) and he became fed up. He bursts out : "Sometimes it stifles me — their business of always hanging together with people like ourselves, all wearing the label *Indian Immigrants*, never daring to try and make contact outside their circle...all our jokes about Indians in England, all our talks about our own situation — never about anyone or anything else. It's so stifling...being aware of who onc is and where one is, God, I am fed up." (188) This upsets his marital life. Sarah feels concerned about it and finds that his "whole personality seemed to be disjointed pieces, rattling together noisily and disharmoniously." (200)

Then he decides to leave England, say good-bye to his phony existence and pretence. He announces it to his wife that he is going "To India-home" and explains to her reasons for doing so.

It is true that his decision to leave England for good was precipitated by the Indo-Pak War of 1965 but the "truth was that his disenchantment with England had began sometime before he read the news in the papers, but this he stowed away in his subconscious, and it was the myth he lived by and acted on." (229) Now the myth is discovered, illusion broken and the disenchanted Adit goes back to his roots, to a place wherefrom none would or could uproot him and the title of the novel assumes its full significance

> Make my bed and light the light,
> I will arrive late tonight.
> Blackbird, bye-bye.

In the novel cross-cultural experience has different effects on different characters. For Adit it is an eye-opener, making him realise the futility of pretension and phoney existence and finally to make him go to India, the country with many ills, nevertheless his own country. For Dev the cross-cultural experience is the beginning of a new life and existence. If Adit completes the full circle, Dev begins a new one. In Adit's case the experience is ironical, for the fire-eater becomes tame and soft. He eats his words and becomes everything that he had pretended, boasted and declared not to be. His case reminds one of a story by Prem Chand, "Nasha" in which Ishwari is like him. Lastly, in case of Sarah the experience culminates into what she had been wishing for, even though she is pained to sever her ties from the land of her birth — "she felt all the pangs of saying good-bye to her past twenty-four years" (221) — the end of her schizophrenic existence, to "enter the real world — whether English or Indian, she did not care, she wanted only its sincerity, its truth." (35) In her case it is Indian, whether good or bad we know not, for the novel ends here and we say, Bye-Bye Blackbird.

NOTE

1. Anita Desai, *Bye-Bye Blackbird* (Delhi : Orient Paperbacks, 1985), p. 18. All future references in this work are incorporated in the body of the article.

4

Kamala Markandaya's *Two Virgins* : A Study in Tradition and Modernity

R.N. RAI

Stephen lgnatius Hemenway has rightly stated that Kamala Markandaya is "definitely one of the most productive, popular and skilled Indo-Anglian novelists and a superb representative of the growing number of Indian women writing serious literature in English."[1] The Russian critic, Kalinnikova, also admits that she is "undoubtedly an outstanding creative artist."[2] She is recognized as a powerful creative writer with the publication of her very first novel *Nectar in a Sieve* in 1954 on account of her fine feminine sensibility, keen observation and a deep sense of involvement in the evolutionary process of Indian society.

Here I am concerned with the evaluation of Mankandaya's eighth novel *Two Virgins*, published in 1973, as this novel has generated a good deal of controversy among the critics regarding its merit as well as demerit. Margaret P. Joseph considers it as the weakest of her novels and nothing more than a documentary about the village life. "There is little attempt", she says, "at plot construction and the story is merely a tedious description of village life, with stereo-typed contrasts between pre- and post-independent India, village and city, traditional Eastern and modern Western ways, the whole amounting to nothing more than a documentary about rural living such as the film director in the novel actually makes."[3] K.S. Ramamurti goes to the extent of saying that *Two Virgins* is a "source of embarrassment for all her admires and critics, for it is not a novel which lives up to the standards set by and the hopes raised in all the earlier novels. It has been considered generally as the poorest of all her works and positively sub-standard too."[4] Though Ramamurti admits that it may be regarded as a novel on the "conflict between the old and the new, the rural and the urban and so on", his main objection is that "there is no consistent exploration nor a convincing fictionalization of any of these themes."[5]

On the other hand, there are such critics as Uma Parameswaran and S. Krishnaswamy who admire this novel for its remarkable characteristics. Uma Parameswaran considers it as a successful novel as it "taps the treasure house of basic human experiences, especially the ever-popular one of adolescence, in a series of well-worded, well-organized vignettes."[6] S. Krishnaswamy finds it remarkable as it "gives us an in-depth study of the problem of growing up into an average woman of an average family in contemporary India."[7] It is true that the novel suffers from the lack of structural compactness, it has merit of its own. It shows the subtle transformation of Indian woman through adolescence into adulthood. It gives us an insight into the concept of 'cultural continuity' in the midst of political, economic and social upheavals. It depicts the changing Indian ethos and reveals Markandaya's "accurate awareness of a gradual shift in values that has been taking place"[8] in post-Independent India. It focuses our attention on the cultural clash between two modes of life, the Eastern and the Western and traces its origin to the very beginning of the process of modernization.

Markandaya is acutely aware of the awakened feminine sensibility in a constantly changing traditional Indian society. She is also aware of the "double pulls that the Indian woman is subject to : between tradition and modernity, between Indian and Western ways of living and values, between her dignity as a human being and her duty as a daughter, wife and mother, between marrying for love and marrying for the mother, between her desire for autonomy and her need for nurture."[9] The eminent feminist author, Simone de Beauvoir, has drawn our attention to the conflict in the female psyche regarding her role as well as the status in contemporary society :

> The women of today are in a fair way to dethrone the myth of feminity; they are beginning to affirm their independence in concrete ways; but they do

> not easily succeed in living completely the life of a human being. Reared by women within a feminine world, their normal destiny is marriage, which still means practically subordination to man; for masculine prestige is far from extinction, resting still upon solid economic and social functions."[10]

Markandaya is mainly concerned with the theme of conflict between traditionalism and modernism, Eastern and Western values and reveals a remarkable variety and profundity within her limited range. Her deep understanding of Eastern and Western values of human life provides her a unique insight into the cultural codes and convictions of different societies. "Like a double-faced Janus", says Harish Raizada, "she can look to both ways of life with keen discernment and dispassionate objectivity."[11] The presence of two cultures in her mind helps her in making a successful quest for real identity.

Though Markandaya's *Two Virgins* is not directly concerned with East-West conflict, it does show "how the modernisms set in by the Western influence incites the protagonists to revolt against their traditional environments and seek their fulfilment by carving their careers independently."[12] The two virgins in the novel are Lalitha and Saroja whose roots are lying deep down in the village life. They are born and brought up in the same environment, but their growing awareness of the adult world and the slow but irresistible encroachment of material values make them move in two different directions. The two spirited young sisters are governed by their own urges and aspirations and react differently to the temptations of the world in which they live.

Lalitha, the elder sister, is prettier than Saroja and is aware of her uncommon beauty. Even Saroja admits the superiority of her beauty "which outclassed that of all these city ladies."[13] She is governed by materialistic considerations, lured by the splendours of the city and therefore rebels against the conservative restrictions of the village life. She is proud of her physical beauty and is willing to lead a luxurious life even through sexual parlance. She is aware of her 'long lustrous eyelashes' and knows when to use them in order to attract a host of admirers. It is evident from the statement of her younger sister, Saroja :

> Lalitha had status. She had no husband yet, but everyone could see when she did she would have more than her fair proportion. There was no rack of emissaries. The young men's mothers sent them, and the women came and spoke to Amma and pinched Lalitha's cheek, and Lalitha was demure, pressed her delicate feet together and cast down her eyes to show off her lashes, which were long and lustrous. Saroja knew it was for show because Lalitha told her.[14]

Lalitha is a liberated girl who feels suffocation in her village surroundings. She aspires for modernity and goes to the extent of violating all norms of traditional Indian society. Her family environment — her Appa, a man of modern outlook and her Amma, a soft and passionate woman, free with her looks and not as pure as Sita or Savitri, and her schooling at Miss Mendosa's Three Kings School nourish individualistic, liberating strains in her personality. She is, therefore, entrapped by a cityhardened, money-encrusted witty entrepreneur, a 'Western punk', Mr. Gupta who exploits her weaknesses by assuring her to give the role of heroine in his film. She is so ambitious that she goes to the city in order to lead a free and independent life. There she is lured by the attractions of the city, seduced by Mr. Gupta and becomes pregnant without marriage. Nothing can be a greater curse than the pre-marital pregnancy for an Indian woman. Indian society does not permit an illegitimate child.

Her parents are forced to take her to the city and try for negotiation with Mr. Gupta who is prepared to pay for the abortion of the child but is not willing to accept her as his wife. There is then no other alternative but to abort the child, though it is extremely shocking to her parents as well as her sister, Saroja. Her father now realises his mistake and repents over his lack of responsibility.

> I educated the milkman, he said, but I couldn't do as much for my own child.... She was innocent, and we let her go out as she was.[15]

Her mother too admits that her lack of control over Lalitha ultimately led her to misery and social disgrace. When Saroja makes a query about the whole truth, she says :

> Your sister wandered too far, she said wearily, she was lured outside the code of our community and is paying the penalty, that is all.[16]

This observation clearly reveals that in her opinion a woman should not go beyond the reasonable limits and should not violate the traditional norms of Indian society. Lalitha's dreams are shattered into pieces simply because she is showy like a comet's tail and her aspirations are based on feminine beauty and sexual liberty. She perhaps does not realise that a woman is bound to be doomed if she gives free rein to what Bhabani Bhattacharya calls "the primeval urge of a woman to be nothing but a woman."[17] She has to face the grim consequences and social ostracisation if she prefers to live only on the sensual plane of existence. Saroja has rightly stated that Lalitha has "more than her fair share of men" and therefore becomes a woman of the street.

Lalitha suffers as she gets herself uprooted from the traditional patterns of Indian society. Like Emma Bovary and Anna Karenina, she has excellent beauty and high expectations from society but ironically ends with utter disillusionment as is evident from the following lines :

> Lalitha who demanded beauty and perfection out of life, who was herself so exquisitely fashioned. But it gave you no claims, none at all, no guarantees whatsoever.[18]

She does not restrain herself and is solely governed by her sexual urges and feminine desirability. Mr. Gupta openly accuses her of being a 'natural' woman : a woman of strong sexual obsession :

> The gist of it was that Lalitha had flung herself at him, he had never been so pestered in his life. Appa, reminded him he was referring to his daughter an innocent and well-brought-up young girl. Mr. Gupta inquired coarsely what she was doing in his studio then, flapping her lashes and issuing invitations to all and sundry.[19]

There is a remarkable thing about the character of Lalitha. Except on one occasion when she makes an attempt to commit suicide by jumping into the well, she does not repent over what she has done.

She rather owns her responsibility in the fatal deed that has been committed :

> It was not his fault alone, it was mine as well, she let fall from bloodless lips.[20]

Whereas Lalitha's mother considers the birth of an illegitimate child as a sin, Saroja is against the abortion of the child, whether legitimate or illegitimate. Lalitha, however, is not much worried over the abortion of the child and advises Saroja not to "cry over spilt milk."[21] She is so daring and unscrupulous that she spurns all the attempts of her parents to rehabilitate her. One morning she disappears from the hotel, leaving her parents for ever, in order to lead her own independent life. In her bedding she tucks a letter which explains her state of mind :

> ....she couldn't face going back to the village; it stifled her, her talents, her ambition. She intended to stay in the city where she belonged. She could look after herself. They weren't to search for her, which in any case would be a waste of time because they would never find her.[22]

Saroja has full sympathy for Lalitha and finds an unending stream from the 'wells of her sorrowing womanhood'. As an innocent village girl she has seen the birth of a baby amidst the milch cows and has assisted Manikkam's wife at the time of her delivery. But the abortion of Lalitha's baby is a shattering blow to the motherly side of her personality. Attaining motherhood is the dream of every woman but, as she realises, motherhood without marriage is a sin and her elder sister Lalitha is paying the penalty for it. Saroja expresses her reaction on this issue like a mature woman :

> If you were married and got pregnant, everyone was pleased except those unfortunate women who were barren. There were little ceremonies to call down blessings on you and when the baby was born everyone came round smiling bringing little presents.... If you weren't married and became pregnant the picture was quite different, it was altogether grim. You hushed it up as best you could and your baby, if ever it got born, had no future at

> all. Saroja thought it wrong : she often mulled about it, especially since her sister, and always reached the same conclusion. It was wrong, a crime against the baby which was the same whether you were married or not, but she knew her elders like Aunt Alamelu who were the majority did not agree.[23]

Aunt Alamelu calls such children as 'fruits of unbridled lust'. Saroja is of the opinion that the life of a woman without the marital yoke, is incomplete. When Lalitha is coming out of the room after the rejection by Mr. Gupta, her remark is very accurate :

> She was like burned-out wood, only just holding her shape.[24]

Marriage is of course essential for the sense of completeness for a woman but Saroja's two reservations are quite pertinent and they cannot be easily ignored. Why should a child, whether legitimate or illegitimate, suffer for no fault of its own? Why should a woman alone pay the penalty for the sin for which man is equally responsible? She gives a subtle hint to the second point in the following lines :

> He sounded quite sorrowful but he wasn't desperate the way Lalitha was, it was his baby but of course he wasn't carrying it.[25]

If Saroja thinks and acts like a mature woman, it does not mean that she does not have the natural instincts of an adolescent girl. She discloses in depth all the unknown, delicate and subtle aspects of feminity through her character. While taking away the glass, when Devaraj touches her hand, she expresses her instinctive reaction :

> When he took his hand away she had the absurd feeling that her skin was rising up to maintain the contact, it couldn't bear to let him go. It reminded her of an experiment in school, iron filings had jumped up like little frenzied men and glued to a magnetized rod. She quelled the feeling instantly, it was too preposterous, but the fire inside refused to die. She wondered if this was what Lalitha had felt like, if it was the cause of her opening herself to him, allowing him to put the seed of the baby inside her.

> It was the only explanation for a girl to be so careless.[26]

Saroja has the natural instinct of a woman and sees in her dream at night what she has thought of in the day about Devraj :

> He lay down beside her and started to caress her. She allowed him to, she discovered she had no sense of shame in revealing, in yielding the shyest, most guarded recesses of her body to him. Each caress was like a passing flame. The sensations were exquisite, were mounting, she could not bear them but she wanted more, she begged him to pierce her entirely and give her peace.[27]

Saroja is keen to know about the details of sexual life. She inquires about it from Chingleput, Jaya and best of all, from Manikkam's wife. She feels immensely delighted in watching the growth of her feminine organs. She is aware of the natural attraction of a girl for a young man but she is fully cautious about its dire consequences. She in fact symbolises the conflict between feeling and reason, innocence and adventure, natural feminine instinct and the social convention, modernity and tradition. At the departure of Devraj her reaction reveals her perceptiveness and deep understanding :

> Saroja longed to run back, fling himself into his arms and tell him she cared although she knew it was hopeless. Instead she followed her parents, which was the proper thing to do. The improper thing was to fling yourself at a man, and she knew what came of that, Lalitha was living evidence. Lalitha, Lalitha. It seemed to Saroja as if her sister was destined to shape the stream of her life.[28]

Saroja is aware of the limitations of a woman which have been forced upon her by the conventions of a traditional society. She can neither philosophise like her father nor forget her sufferings in drinks like the men folk. Saroja is quite emphatic on this issue in her statement :

> Women had no boltholes. There was no escape for them, they had to stand where they were and take it.[29]

Saroja is aware of this fact that suppression of woman has been a constant phenomenon since time immemorial. All the rules and restrictions have been formulated just to hinder the natural growth of the woman. She considers society as the 'beastly tamer'. She is, however, not in favour of the radical transformation of society. She believes that emancipation of woman is but a slow evolutionary process.

Saroja behaves like a sensible and intelligent girl. She observes acutely, learns her lesson quietly and takes a decision wisely. She knows that a liaison with Mr. Devraj would not give any respectably position to her in society. That is why in the process of appeasing her, when Devraj comes close to her and touches her, she reacts sharply :

> Saroja leapt up. Her flesh was molten. She knew what he was asking. She knew where it ended. She had dragged her bloated gravid sister out of the bag, she had seen the bloody pulp of the baby.

And therefore she asks :

> What do you take me for, she screamed, a virgin in your whorehouse?[30]

Saroja acts like a mature woman of firm conviction. She is so pragmatic in outlook that Devraj with urban attraction or Chingleput with rural affection cannot tempt her into the sexual trap. Though she knows that she can never be a match to Lalitha in physical appearance and can therefore never command her parents' similar affection, she has full regard for them and is not hostile to any one.

Saroja is deeply rooted in her village culture as she believes that one dies if one's roots are destroyed. She has great fascination for home as well as for village life. She, therefore, requests her parents to go back to the village as in the village "there were fields to rest your eyes on, colors that changed with the seasons. The tender green of new crops, the tawny shades of harvest, the tints of fleshly turned earth, you could have told the week and the month of the year by these alone. You knew each grove, each acre, each homestead on it — You always knew where you were. You knew who you were."[31]

Saroja is willing to lead a natural, intimate and affectionate life. In her opinion city life symbolises artificial life, as in the city people hanker after money and lose their own identity. She feels disgusted with the city life as she does not want to pass through "the stifling, bewildering, terrible streets of thiy hideous maze."[32] Moreover in the city "you were one in a hundred, in a thousand, you were no longer you, you might have been an amoeba. You drifted, amoeba like, through the baffling streets, wondering where you were, what business you had.... You stood, buffeted, like a tree in a storm, like some stubborn tedious obstruction people implied, their looks, their sighs, their jabbing elbows were eloquent."[33]

The novel presents the contrast between tradition and modernity, between rural and the urban way of living and thinking. If Lalitha stands for extreme modernity, Aunt Alamelu stands for extreme conservatism. Aunt Alamelu considers Miss Mendoza's ways as 'modern'. Lalitha as 'cosmopolitan'. Their Appa is also Western in thinking, as he wants "Indian to be Westernized, which advanced them into the big world instead of remaining static in a backwater."[34] Saroja, who is the central character, represents the balance. Though she is aware of the feminine sensibility and the suppression of woman in society, she is so deeply rooted in Indian culture that she prefers to live within the traditional patterns of Indian society. The following lines clearly reveal the deep contrasts between the attitude of Saroja and Lalitha :

> She wanted lots of lovely cuddly babies, and as Appa said, the way society was organized you had to be married for that. A peasant's ambition, Lalitha called it, but Saroja did not feel herself demeaned by that, there were lots of qualities to peasants that she greatly admired.[35]

Saroja uses bicycle in spite of the protests from Aunt Alamelu, likes to read in the English School of Miss Mendoza and wants to live in the pleasant company of Chingleput but she does not cross the threshold of Indian womanhood. She has been able to achieve a wonderful synthesis of Eastern and Western values in human life. The implied message in the novel is that India should not discard her great traditional values and forget her glorious past just for the immediate splendours of the West. She should not, however, stick to her obsolete values.

The greatness of the novel also lies in the use of different images with symbolic implications. Butterflies symbolise the charming girls and bats stand for the unscrupulous city people like Mr. Gupta who were responsible for the exploitation and degradation of women like Lalitha who is described as 'flower-fresh' and 'a mangled flower in the darkness'. Moods of different characters have been represented by employing different weather conditions. The dove-eagle image expresses the central theme of the novel. While welcoming Mr. Gupta Lalitha draws 'a Colam pattern in saffron and white' which symbolises dove. Mr. Gupta shuffles his feet and the dove gets blurred. Lalitha kneels, brushes away the scuffed powder and finds "a eagle, a golden eagle soaring over the plains."[36] The symbolic implication is that dove-like Lalitha loses her chastity simply because she has soaring ambition like an eagle. She wants to reach the height which is beyond her limit and hence suffering becomes inevitable.

REFERENCES

1. Stephen Ignatius Hemenway, *The Novel of India*, Vol. II (Calcutta : Writers Workshop, 1975), p. 52.
2. Elena J. Kalinnikova, *Indian English Literature : A Survey* (Ghaziabad : Vimal Prakashan, 1982), p. 163.
3. Margaret P. Joseph, *Kamala Markandaya* (New Delhi : Arnold-Heinemann, 1980), pp. 79-80.
4. K.S. Ramamurti, "Two Virgins" : A Problem Novel, *Perspectives on Kamala Markandaya* ed. Madhusudan Prasad (Ghaziabad : Vimal Prakashan, 1984), p. 198.
5. *Ibid.*, p. 199.
6. Uma Parameswaran, *A Study of Representative Indo-English Novelists* (New Delhi : Vikas Publishing House, 1976), p. 121.
7. S. Krishnaswamy, *The Woman in Indian Fiction in English* (New Delhi : Ashish Publishing House, 1984), p. 163.
8. Shiv K. Kumar, "Tradition and Change in the Novels of Kamala Markandaya", *Osmania Journal of English Studies,* Vol. VIII, No. 1, 1969, p. 1.
9. S. Krishnaswamy, *The Woman in Indian Fiction in English*, p. 354.
10. Simone de Beauvoir, Introduction to Book Two, *The Second Sex,* trans. and ed. by H.M. Parshley (Harmondsworth : Penguin, 1979), p. 30.

11. Harish Raizada, "East-West Confrontation in the Novels of Kamala Markandaya", *Perspectives on Kamala Markandaya* ed. Madhusudan Prasad, p. 37.
12. *Ibid.*, p. 50.
13. Kamala Markandaya, *Two Virgins* (Delhi : Vikas Publishing House Pvt. Ltd., 1975), p. 211.
14. *Ibid.*, p. 13.
15. *Ibid.*, p. 178.
16. *Ibid.*, p. 234.
17. Bhabani Bhattacharya, *Shadow from Ladakh* (New Delhi : Hind, 1966), p. 274.
18. Kamala Markandaya, *Two Virgins*, pp. 229-30.
19. *Ibid.*, p. 219.
20. *Ibid.*, p. 178.
21. *Ibid.*, p. 233.
22. *Ibid.*, p. 236.
23. *Ibid.*, p. 201.
24. *Ibid.*, p. 220.
25. *Ibid.*, p. 219.
26. *Ibid.*, p. 218.
27. *Ibid.*, p. 227.
28. *Ibid.*, p. 221.
29. *Ibid.*, p. 123.
30. *Ibid.*, p. 245.
31. *Ibid.*, p. 243.
32. *Ibid.*
33. *Ibid.*, pp. 243-44.
34. *Ibid.*, p. 57.
35. *Ibid.*, pp. 57-58.
36. *Ibid.*, p. 108.

5

Religion, Sex and Politics in Salman Rushdie's *The Satanic Verses*

PRAMOD KUMAR SINGH

Salman Rushdie has established himself as one of the best novelists of the world. With just six novels — *Grimus*, *Midnight's Children*, *Shame*, *The Satanic Verses*, *The Moor's Last Sigh* and *The Ground Beneath Her Feet* to his credit, he has emerged as a major novelist delineating the contemporary scene on the Indian Sub-continent. His latest novel *The Moor's Last Sigh* and *The Ground Beneath Her Feet* has recently been refused the literary fiction Award of 1996 for depicting in the novel some irrelevant sex scenes which features such choice phrases as "Uma, my Uma, murmured in my ear near the Everest of our ecstasy on the south of col of desire." Very few of the readers know that *The Satanic Verses* also contains many sex scenes, apparently irrelevant to the plot, interlinked with elements of religion.

The novel *The Satanic Verses* is a fine allegory. Rushdie has used dream within-a-dream concept throughout the novel. The subject matter of the novel is fairly varied and several stories are interlinked with each other to form the whole context of the plot. The stories contained in the novel are neither stereo-typed nor predictable. The novel often arouse the feelings of disgust among the readers, not just because of gratuitously offensive remark against the prophet of Islam, Hindu's God Hanuman and holy 'Koran', but also for several sex scenes spreading over the different parts of the novel.

Rushdie does not hesitate to name his characters quite identical to the real names. He used the name "Mohound" in stead of the widely accepted "Mohammad". He uses other religious names such as Hamaza, Ayesha, Ganesh, Hanuman etc. in its real form. The battles which the prophet Mohammad had to win in order to convert people were very real. All characters like the 'Lat' and 'Mant' are the part of Islamic folklore. Rushdie however accepts the truth that his personal knowledge of Islamic culture and religion has come into his fictional imagination.

> "Actually, one of my major themes is religion and fanaticism. I have talked about the Islamic religion because that is what I know the most about. But the ideas about religious faith and nature of religious experience and also the political implications of religious extremism are applicable with a few variations to just about any religion. In the beginning and the end of the novel there are other kinds of fundamentalism also.[1]

The novel presents mirror images of some religious places. The place Jahilia, the city of sand, is shown to suffer when the camel trains start losing their business to the boats and the ruler Abu Simbel is convinced that "Only the pilgrimage stands between the city and its ruin." The council, therefore, searches the world for "statutes of alien gods, to attract new pilgrims." But there is no mere competition as "down in Sheba a great temple has been built, a shrine to rival the house of black stone". The rulers have no choice but to add "the tempting spices of profanity to their religious practices".

Oscillating between the koranic past and the present, the past throws torch-light on the absurdities of the present. Ayesha, the youngest and most desirable of Mohound's twelve wives, appears in the middle of the book living chastely in the harem quarters of the great mosque at Yathrib. She reappears in the several chapters and centuries later, clad only in butterflies, to lead entire village into the Arabian sea. The sea is expected to part and the pilgrims to go straight to Mecca. The root idea of the novel seems that there is no absolute and the heaven and the Hell have no boundaries. It is almost impossible to tell angel and devil apart. Mohound, the prophet, has a tough time telling the difference between the voice of the angel and the shaitan (devil) on the Mount Coney. In the process, Rushdie takes a very irrelevant look at Islamic folklore and Koranic facts.

Besides the prophet of Islam, Rushdie has depicted the Hindu's religious gods and Christian's folklore as well. He seems to be totally devoid of any religious respect while depicting muslim and non-muslims, gods and goddess. It appears very sinister when the prophet Mohound is seen in extra-marital affair with Grandee's wife in a sacred religious place. The Grandee's wife endeavours to justify her illicit relation by saying that her husband is "a weak man."

> Don't say anything, Mohound. I am Grandee's wife, and neither of us is your friend. My husband, however, is a weak man. In Jahilia they think he's cunning, but I know better. He knows I take lovers and he does nothing about it, because the temples are in my family's care. Lat's uzza's Manat's. The shall I call them Mosque". (p. 120)

In chapter two, Rushdie refers to a prophet born in a desert which is obviously about the Christian's god "Lord Jesus Christ". The birth of the prophet is very much similar to the actual birth story of Jesus Christ. The name of the mother *i.e.* Maryam, is also the same.

> "A prophet, Isa, born to a woman named Maryam, born of no man under a palm-tree in the desert, stories that made his eyes shine, then fade into a distanceness". (p. 118)

Gibreel Farrista, a character, is a famous hero of religious films of Bombay. He is shown to role the character of Lord 'Ganesh'. The hero was shown to be in avalanche of sex. He had so many sexual partners that it was not uncommon for him to forget their names even before they had left his room. After the Gibreel played the role of Ganesh in six movies, he became so popular that many young ladies asked him if he would keep the Ganesh mask on his face while they made love with him but he refuse out to respect for the dignity of the god. Consequently Rekha, the wife of a ball-bearing manufacturer, also comes into his contact and undergo extra-marital relations. When Rekha found betrayed in her love, she abuses him by calling "lafanga", "haramzada", "salah" and also "accused him of fucking the sister".

In one part of the novel, Abraham takes his wife Hagar into the wilderness and leaves her there. She asks him as to whether it is a

God's will. Abraham answers in positive and at this point Rushdie refers him as the bastard. Rushdie also shows that there is a Jahilia, a tent of Black stone called 'The curtain', where twelve prostitutes named as twelve wives of Mohound are shown. The eldest was of fifty and the youngest among the girl was of fifteen. The girls used to talk on vulgar topics including money, sex, fucking etc. Rushdie has shown them in sex in very disgusting ways;

> "out of working hours they would tease him deliciously, flaunting their bodies before them, placing their breasts against his lips, twining their legs around his waist, kissing one another passionately just an inch away from his face, until the ashy writer was hopelessly aroused." (p. 379)

Rushdie holds the faith of reincarnation common in almost all religions. Buddhists believe that the soul of former Lama transmigrated into Lama after demise of old religious guru. Lord Vishnu who undergone several rebirth, are found in Christian's mythology also. In the first chapter, Rushdie affirms the belief of rebirth common in all religions by depicting Lord Vishnu, Dalai Lama and Jesus Christ :

> "Reincarnation, for frenzied Gibreel, was term beneath whose shield many nations gather a babbling; phoenix-from ashes, the resurrection of Christ, the transmigration, at the instances of death, of the soul of Dalai Lama into the body of a new-born child...such matter to mix up with the avtars of Vishnu." (p. 84)

The extra-marital relations are not bad for Salman Rushdie. Rushdie does not see anything wrong in even holding an illegitimate child. In chapter five, we see how Mishal Sufyan under go illicit sexual relation just because her husband was unable to provide a child. She deliberately avoids contraceptive precautions to become pregnant. She is not ashamed at all to hold the 'immature bastard' in her womb. In chapter three, Jumpy Joshi is seen in immoral acts with a widow Pamella Chamcha. Although Rushdie chooses to write on Indian subcontinent and characters yet sometimes completely ignore social norms of the place. This is the reason that Pamella, despite being a lady, take out two bottles of wine and drink with her lover

Jumpy Joshi before making love with him. She was further seen totally dry-eyed and composed after hearing the message of her husband's demise in a plane accident which is absolutely an abnormal conduct for a widow.

Rushdie is aware of social inequality in Indian Society. He highlights the problem of untouchability among Hindus. He shows how lower caste people called schedule caste are put to humiliations by upper caste men. Many schedule caste people change their religion out of frustration. Even naming them as 'children of God' do not instill any sense of social security and respect among them. Rushdie in *The Satanic Verses* depicts as to how the lower castemen are not allowed to fetch water from the village's common well. He ironically says that these water-tight social divisions are the main cause of social tensions in Indian society. This is reason that Osman in chapter four, decides to relinquish Hindu religion and accepts Islam as he thinks that it would do good for him. Rushdie's tone is not less pungent than Mulk Raj Anand's *Untouchable* while highlighting the plights of lower caste people and social unequality in Indian social milieu.

Rushdie deals almost every aspects of society confronting a common man in day to day life. Politics is his prime concern and almost every novel deals political issues at length. Rushdie thinks that politics has invaded every walk of life in our society. This is the reason that the prime concern of Salman Rushdie in his all novels, except *Grimus*, is political happenings of Indian sub-continent. His novels deal with almost major political happenings of India, Pakistan and Bangladesh. Emergency in India, Bangladesh liberation war, national movement, politics of Shiv Sena in Bombay, Kashmir problem, social inequality, Muslim league — almost every major political events are discussed at length. All important political figures Indira Gandhi, General Zia, Rajiv Gandhi, N.T. Rama Rao, M.G.R., Amitabh Bachan, etc. are conspicuous in the novel. Rushdie explain in an interview with *The Gentleman* (Feb. 1994) as to why he has chosen to write on politics :

> "I am a fairly political animal. I do think that when you include political material in fiction, it creates special problem. I think a lot of what I have written to do with public affairs and I am interested in that.

> But it must also be possible to write books that have nothing to do with politics. It is getting harder, I suspect, because politics invades our lives these days in a way that it once didn't."[2] (p. 59)

Rushdie was condemned world-wide for misrepresenting Islam and interpreting Koranic messages. In the chapter six, the death of prophet is described and the last words put into his mouth are his thanks to the heathen goddess Al Lal. This is offensive to an average muslim fundamentalist as would be a fictional account of Mahatma Gandhi's death, where it be suggested that, hit by the assassin's bullet, he exclaimed (instead of Hai Ram) "get me ox soup". The reference to prophet Mohammad's wives as prostitute was the gravest offensive act. Rushdie, however, denies the charges in a recent interview in *The Mail* (June 18, 1989) and says, "there are a lot of specific accusations against *The Satanic Verses* for instance that I've called prophet's wives prostitutes which actually I haven't. Another is that I have used the name Mohound, Pejorative of Mohammad".[3] (p. 2)

Rushdie's references to Hindu's gods and mythological legends are completely devoid of respects. The readers of the novel often confront with names such as Hanuman, Gautam, Krishna, Vishnu Ramayan etc. Lord Krishna's indulgence of romance with Gopis are referred in the novel without any fictional change. Rushdie characterises Gibreel, who acts as 'Lord Ganesh' in films, to be a man of easy virtue and this can obviously offend a pious Hindu. "He had so many sexual partners that it was uncommon for him to forget their names even before they had left his room." (p. 25) Rushdie compares Lord Krishna with Lord Buddha (Gautam) who meditated up to utmost human suffering beneath a 'Bodhi-tree'.

The novel has erupted volcanic protests throughout the world mainly because Rushdie has used some insulting words for Mohammad's wives and even Mohammad himself was depicted in the novel as a man of loose character. The wives of Mohammads, while living in the harem, were shown to talk about money, fucking and sex. Their indulgence in sex is also abnormal. The young girls of harem were sometimes referred sarcastically as butterflies. Some words and phrases such as "butterflies", "asking to be consumed" also ironically bear the double meanings.

Rushdie, however, cannot be, despite all controversies regarding his fictional writings, regarded as a "communal rabble rouser nor a motivated politician but a person who deserves respect as a writer of uncommon talent."[4] *The Satanic Verses* is his outstanding literary achievement. The banning of *Shame* in Pakistan and now *The Satanic Verses* in India and other countries is nothing but the manifestation of a world-wide trend by which authorities have made all forms of art, a classic target or censorship. The basic objective of censorship is not only to suppress the work of art but also bureaucratically criminalize the creative imagination. Some critics say to this extent that Rushdie deliberately arouses the controversies in his novels inviting banning of the books. This is because banned books always get more attentions and their circulation increases tremendously. It is further stated that Salman Rushdie has signed a 850,000 pounds contract with the publishers, a handsome amount, and the publisher who invests so much wants to get maximum publicity through such international controversy.

REFERENCES

1. Salman Rushdie, *The Satanic Verses* (Penguin Books Limited, London, 1988).
2. Salman Rushdie, An Interview with *The Gentleman,* February, 1994, p. 59.
3. Salman Rushdie, An Interview with *The Mail*, London, June 18, 1989.
4. "The Controversial Rushdie", *The Times of India* (October 30, 1988).

6

Marital Discord in R.P. Jhabvala's Fiction

JAGDISH PRASAD SINGH

R.P. Jhabvala is a prestigious name in Indian Fiction today. Married to a Parsi gentleman, Jhabvala came to India as a young and beautiful wife of Cyrus Jhabvala a young Parsi architect. Coming over to India, the creative artist in Jhabvala observed, "As a writer I consider myself exceedingly fortunate to have come here when I did and the way I did."[1] Her-first experiences of the Indian social situation find full descriptions in her novels. On first looking at the Indian soil she came out with the following remarks : "It came about instinctively. I was enraptured. I felt I understood India so well. I loved everything."[2] The words as enraptured, love and excitement are suggestive of her personal attachment to India and the Indian people. By 1960 she has published her four novels *To Whom She Will* (1955), *The Nature of Passion* (1956), *Esmond In India* (1957) and *The House Holder* (1960). After her short stay in Britain she came out with her fifth novel *Get Ready for Battle* (1962). She received the prestigious Bookers award for her novel *Heat & Dust*. Having spent 24 years in India she presents in her fiction the minute details of the people and places and their problems. The problem of marital discord is portrayed in almost all her novels and her characters pass through crisis after crisis and most of them are in quest of better partner searching their hearts within. In this paper it is attempted to expose to the readers the marital discord in the central characters of Jhabvala.

The institution of marriage based on social system to satiate the inborn urge of sex is of utmost importance. The concept of marriage is age old and has been popular and prevalent in human society since time immemorial. Thus, marriage is practically universal social tie, though it is regarded as an obstacle and hurdle in all adventures of life. The principle of marriage and its practice based on free choice of the boys and girls are only popular in the western world. In India, it is used for strengthening relationship or for creating new alliances but in no case the decision to marry a particular person rests with a boy or a girl. In this way marriage in India is a sacred bond to tie truly two souls together. It remains an infinite bond of two souls from life to life and birth to birth.

Jhabvala's first novel to whom she will has the very striking theme of marital discord. Amrita and Hari the two major characters, show the contrasting opinions about the institution of the arranged marriage. The novel opens with the following lines : "for if she bids a maiden still she gives herself to whom she will, then marry her in tender age so warns the heaven begotten sage."[3] Hari, the unheroic hero, is emotionally squashed under the protective love of his family. It is through the character of Hari that the novelist shows the ideological control of his family over the individual who is bound to follow its standards and norms. Hari hails from a typical middle class family who has settled in Delhi after partition. He is a weak man who finds it difficult to protest either against the wishes and whims of his family or those of his beloved Amrita. He lacks courage and confidence, self-determination and will power. He is over-powered by his emotional and romantic ideas. He falls in love with Amrita, a Delhi station artist and has a desire to marry her. But as a laggard in her, he finds it impossible to go against the wishes of his family. When Krishna Sen Gupta asks him if he cared more for his family than his beloved, he very cleverly avoids this question. He ultimately deserts Amrita and marries Sushila. Hari's dilemmas : "Decide always now a day from all sides it was decided",[4] show his undecisive character. The matrimonial discord comes to the forefront when Hari's final surrender to the decision of his family is complete.

Amrita, the heroine of the novel typifies self-determination in marriage. She is practical and sensible and has revolted against her dominating mother Radha. Marriage to her is a purely personal matter. She is self-willing so much so that she acts as she desires.

She tells Hari : "What does my family matter you know? I would give up every one and everything for you. Nothing matters only you."[5] Her own family as well as that of Hari is equally insignificant for her. After meeting Prema, Hari's sister, she shows the same spirit of caring a fig for any one and persuades even Hari to have such an attitude : "But O Hari even if your sister does not like me, even your whole family does not like me, what will it matter? They cannot come between us. They are no more important than my family, they will never be able, to separate us."[6] She is self-willed, bold and active like Isabel Archer in Henry James' *The Portrait of a Lady* or like Elizabeth Bennet in Jane Austine's *Pride and Prejudice*. The end of the novel is indeed very significant. The novelist allows Hari to marry Sushila and Amrita marries Krishna Sen Gupta.

In *The Nature of Passion* the novelist once again lays stress on community feeling among Indians which results into marital discord. She shows how the member of Laljee's family disapprove the Nemi's action of having an affair with parsi boy, a boy belonging to a different community. The whole family can never develop good relation with Laljee's daughter-in-law Kanta who comes from a different community. Laljee's sister always taunts him for allowing his son to marry outside the community and whenever Kanta fails to perform her duty as a daughter-in-law, her behaviour is explained in these words : "I know very well what happens when people marry outside the community."[7] The novelist shows that in most of cases of arranged marriages discord is noticeable. It is because of the fact that in today's set up of society, dowry is bane, the dangerous devil of dowry has devoured many dear daughter of their parents. It is fully and freely demanded and unwillingly given by the parents of the bride. It is a kind of high premium paid for an insured life for a bride, in the groom's house. The higher the groom in status and rank, the bigger is the premium of the dowry. The novelist does not give her personal remarks against dowry but leaves it to the judgment and sensibility of the reader. In *The Nature of Passion* Laljee will give dowry and no one in Delhi will believe the figure.

The same theme of matrimonial discord is repeated time and again in the novels of Jhabvala, posing a particular disharmony. In her next novel in *Esmond In India* she repeats this popular theme of disharmony in cross cultural marriage. The novelist describes the marriage relationship of Gulab, a rich Indian girl with Esmond. She crops deeper into Esmond's weakness as an European and also Gulab's short-comings as a traditional Indian. There are difference in their food habits, tastes, likings and dislikings. Esmond is upset by the spicy smell of rich food which is liked by Gulab. He is displeased with Gulab's living patterns. The novelist observes. "He, Esmond is crude and even offensive. His sarcasm, his sneer, his contempt is all lost on Gulab since with her pretty looks she is very languorous and placid."[8] Ultimately Gulab leaves Esmond and thus an autumnal curtain is drawn over dry, dull, disharmonious and discordant relationship with Esmond.

The novelist presents another case of disharmony in married life in *Get Ready for Battle*. Guljari Lal and Sarla Devi are couple married for a many years. They live a married life full of dissonance and disturbance. Sarla Devi is so-called social worker. She does not live with her husband who believes in money making morality and leads a materialistic life. Another pair in this novel is Vishnu and Mala. Mala is frank, forward and fashionable woman but she does not like that her husband should mix up with unmarried girls and a number of hooked woman. Thus, it is amply demonstrated in the fiction of Jhabvala that marital discord is the central theme of many of her novels.

REFERENCES

1. R. Agrawal, "An Interview with *Ruth Prawer Jhabvala*" *Quest*; 91 (1974), p. 36.
2. ''A Novelist of India reflects two worlds'', *New York Times*, Tuesday, 17th July 1973, Author unnamed.
3. R.P. Jhabvala, *To Whom She Will*, London : George Allen and Unwin Ltd., 1955.
4. *Ibid.*, p. 175.
5. *Ibid.*, p. 29.
6. *Ibid.*, p. 32.
7. *The Nature of Passion* (London : George Allen and Unwin Ltd., 1956), p. 80.
8. *Esmond In India* (London : George Allen & Unwin Ltd., 1957), p. 97.

7

Feminism in R.K. Narayan's Novels

SIYARAM PRASAD SINHA

R.K. Narayan is a novelist of international repute. His novels are the clorama for the changing Indian society and present the microcosmic India caught in the crucible of tradition and change. His novels mirror the intimate pictures of Indian Society and the characters are the reflections of real people. Narayan is the minute observer of society presenting most realistic pictures charged with gentle irony and light humour. His approach to the subject-matter is always marked with intellectual inspirations and his artistic excellence lies in authentic exploration of social problems.

Narayan, living absorbed in religion and family, is quite familiar with the developments within an Indian family. "The family is the immediate context in which his sensibility operates and novels are remarkable for subtlety and conviction with family relationships are treated."[1] His novel *The English Teacher* (1945) is a fine peep into "a little middle class home and the comic irony of the petty problems of the daily business of living".[2] The novel highlights the plight and predicament of a common housewife in Indian family.

The heroine of *The English Teacher* Sushila, like a common housewife, is victim of exploitation in the men dominated society. Narayan ironically says in the novel that the women's economic dependence on men is the prime cause of domestic discords in Indian families. Although Constitution of India has enshrined equal rights to women and men, yet a pervasive dichotomy prevails between the theory and practice of these rights and privileges. In fact, a woman is always on the mercy of her husband throughout her life. Savitri therefore, rightly reacts in *The Dark Room* and says :

> "Women don't possess anything in the world. What possession can a woman call her own except her body. Everything else that she has in her father's, husband's, or her son's. (p. 75)

Nayaran brings out the qualities of an ideal house-wife in *The English Teacher*. The heroine Sushila is replica of a devoted Hindu wife for whom her family and her domestic duty comes first. She is an apt cash-keeper. She appears Krishnan to be a ruthless accountant that a hundred rupees seemed to do the work of two hundred, and all throughout the month she was able to give money whenever Krishnan requires.

Sushila wants to "Save money" for the future of her baby as she knows that a girl is liability for the parents of Hindu society. The parents, soon after the birth of a girl child, start worrying for her marriage. They save money to arrange dowry for the child's marriage. Like every mother of the Indian society, Sushila also worries for the daughter's wedding. She suggests her husband, "When we are old we must never trouble others for her. And remember there is a daughter, for whose marriage we must save." (p. 46)

Some minor discords often occur in the matrimonial life of a woman and a man. Narayan shows us as to how such differences sometimes develops between the wife and husband on flimsy matters. Although the matrimonial relation of Krishnan and Sushila is supremely happy, yet a minor strife takes place in between them when Sushila sells an old watch. They did not talk each other for a while but soon their pride fumbled and prejudice dissolved like Darcy and Elizabeth of *Pride and Prejudice*. Such understanding lacks in the case of Rosie and Marco, her husband in *The Guide* and hence Raju succeeds to slip into their life.

In *The Dark Room*, Narayan utilizes the Savitri's familiar pattern of domestic disharmony to sketch the status of women in Indian society. The women are helpless victim of exploitation and hence when Savitri leaves her home, she is shown to be exploited also by the temple priest where she takes shelter. Sharing the agony and anguish of all helpless Hindu wives, Savitri expressed her feelings by making a fiery speech, "I'm a human being. You men will never grant that. For you we are playthings when you feel like hugging and slaves at other time. Don't think that you can fondle us when you like and kick us when you choose". (p. 73) Savitri further highlights the anguish of women by saying that "What is the difference between a prostitute and married women ? The prostitute changes her men but a married women does not. That's all; but both earn their food and shelter in the same manner." (p. 76)

Narayan shows us as to how the husband is like a god in the Indian household and women have to accept whatever fate has destined to them. This is the reason that the priest in charge of the temple gives suggestion : "If she won't let rest, thrash her, that is the way to keep women sane. In these days you fellow are mugs, and let your women ride you about." (p. 109) And Savitri therefore feels that nothings is her own and even her children are her husband's absolutely : "You paid the mid-wife and the nurse. You pay for their cloths and teachers. You are right. Didn't I say that a woman owns nothings". (p. 77) And furthermore the cart driver of *The Painter of Signs* tends to thrash her wife if she disobeys him or Ramani's cook in *The Dark Room* who "nearly broke her (wife's) bone" for a minor thing. R.S. Singh rightly says, "Here is the sort of thing that happens in thousands of households in our country; a few Savitris hang, burn or drown themselves. The great majority dare not to do it".[3]

Savitri represents thousands of other Indian housewives who are helpless creatures in the hands of their husbands. When Savitri prevents her son from going to school due to illness, she is worsted and humiliated by her husband : "mind your own business, do you hear. Go and do any work you like in the kitchen but leave the training of a grown up to him. It is none of a woman's business". (p. 5) Savitri woefully thinks about her existence : "How important at home, and that after fifteen years of married life". (p. 8) This state of helplessness is the case of other housewives also who lead their life under the complete dominance of their husbands. The social status of an Indian housewife is evaluated at the end of the novel. The plight of women is reflected from the Savitri's version "What despicable creation of God are we that we can't exist without a support. I am like a bamboo pole which cannot stand without a wall to support it".[4] (p. 113)

We thus arrive at a conclusion that Narayan is a minute observer of society and shows all minor events which an ordinary eye is prone to miss. He probes into the everyday incidents in Hindu Households of Indian Society and exposes the predicament of common housewives. The heroines typify all suffering housewives of our society who are exploited by all means in their life. His novels depict the ironies of modern Indian life where women on one hand are regarded as 'Devi' (goddess) and on the other hand are deprived of their basic rights.[5]

NOTES

1. William Walsh, ''Indian Novelists In English'', *The Times of India*, Oct. 2, 1965.
2. M.K. Naik, *The Ironic Vision* (Sterling Publishers Pvt. Ltd., Delhi, 1983), p. 23.
3. R.S. Singh, *The Indian Novel In English* (Arnold-Heinemanm, New Delhi, 1977), p. 62.
4. R.K. Narayan, *The Dark Room* (Orient Paperbacks, New Delhi).
5. R.K. Narayan, *The English Teacher* (India Thought Publication, Mysore).

8

Salman Rushdie's Novels : Themes & Techniques

PRAMOD KUMAR SINGH AND MRS. ROMA SINGH

Salman Rushdie, a Bombay born London-based novelist, ranks among the world's best contemporary novelists like Milan Kundera, Gracia Marquez, Gunter Grass, John Irving and V.S. Naipaul. His novel *Midnight's Children* (1980) has unleashed the torrent of praise when it won the 1981 Booker Maconnall Prize. Rushdie's two novels — *Grimus* (1975) and *Shame* (1983) have also shown a kind of talent found in world-class novelist. *The Satanic Verses* (1988) finally made Rushdie the best-known writer of the world; though forced him to live in fugitives under heavy security since Iran's spiritual leader Late Ayatollah Khomeini called for his death for his alleged blasphemy in the novel.

Rushdie's first novel *Grimus* (1975) is endowed with mushroom magic images. There are some confusing rock-like creatures called gorfs in the novel. They riddle human minds with anagrams, phantasmogoric time travel with a stone rose that makes things materialize out of thin air. That the first part of the novel leaves us slightly confused, wondering whether we are going to find our bearings. We are further caught in parables about utopia and life. Flapping Eagle, is the hero of the novel who swallow the elixir of mortality and wanders the face of the earth for ever. He sees things "Most men miss in a mere life time" but one day exclaims, "I want to grow old, not to die but to grow old." He later falls form his yacht and passes through a hole in the sea and is washed ashore in calf island. The mythical world of calf island is populated by people who have drunk the elixir of mortality. *Grimus* is rather a difficult novel for a common reader and differs entirely from his later novels. *Grimus*, as Rushdie himself says, was started by him when he was just ten years old and was finished in 1979.

In *Midnight's Children* (1980), Rushdie seems to be talking about politics in a style similar to that of the Chech writer Milan Kundra. The plot of *Grimus* (1975) is more a historical, whereas *Midnight's Children* (1980) is more on the lines of a Bildungsroman (a novel from dealing with a person's early development) like R.K. Narayan's *Swami and Friends* and Gunter Grass's *Tin Drum*. The hero of the novel Saleem was born on the stroke of midnight and hence the novel was named as *Midnight's Children*. The novel is called as "autobiographical" as the hero Saleem and Rushdie were born in the same part of the city Bombay and at the same time. In the novel, there is a direct collision with the individual with history. It is the moment in Indian history in which Saleem spent his childhood claiming that he, in some way, can influence his great historical events. The Bangladesh liberation movement and Emergency in India have greatly influenced the theme of the novel. The part-III of the novel is direct and more political book than the earlier parts of the book.

Shame (1983), banned in Pakistan, is different from Rushdie's earlier books. At that times, he shows tendency to upstage the plot with his own presence. *Shame* contains a number of stories, each story is somehow interlinked with each other. Commenting about the novel Rushdie says, "I don't feel that while writing *Shame* or *Midnight's Children*, I discovered myself as a political novelist. It seems to me that everything in both book has to do with politics and with the relation of the individuals and history. In fact, both *Shame* and *Midnight's Children* closely follow the parallels or thematic patterns. The role of Omar Khayyam Shakil in the novel *Shame* is identical with that of Saleem Sinai in the *Midnight's Children*. Both novels represent Rushdie's satirical venom applied with merciless comic vituperation to the political reportage of scenario in the two countries. And both are supremely grotesque vehicles for linking fanciful family-tale and murky political history. Omar is an unspeakable personality, fat and ugly and scandalous, an inverted rascal of a voyeur who took advantage of gullible women in the guise of mesmeric medical treatment, and married unspeakably to a beauty that was also a beat, with a child's mind in a woman's body; raise by three mothers. *Shame* seems to contain within itself two stories which eventually mingle with Omar Khayyam who is probably the most withdrawn character in fiction. But there is also the other story where the two most important men in Pakistan's recent history become the central protagonists. The most offending part of *Shame* is perhaps beginning of the Chapter-VII, where Rushdie mentions the incident of a Pakistani father who murdered his only daughter because she made love to a white boy and says that the story appalled him because he found himself sympathising with the killer.

The Satanic Verses (1988), thematically based on Islamic history, is an unequivocal attack on religious fundamentalism. Speaking about the novel, says Rushdie, "Actually, one of my major themes in religion and fanaticism. I have talked about the Islamic religious because that is what I know that most about. But the ideas about religious faith and the nature of religious experiences and also the political implications of religious extremism is applicable with a few variations just about my religion." In the beginning and the end of the novel, there are other kinds of fundamentalism also. The novel opens with a bang a hijacked Air India Jumboo; Boston 420 explodes over England. The only two survivors are India's Film heroes, Gibreel Farissta and Saladin Chamcha, the expatriate Brown Uncle Tom. The root idea of the novel is that there is no absolute in the universe. There is no boundary between Heaven and Hell. It's almost impossible to differentiate angel and devil apart. Even the prophet Mohound has a tough time telling the difference between the voice of the angel and the devil (Saitan) up there on Mount Coney. Thus, Rushdie takes a very irrelevant look at Islamic as well as Hindu folklores in the novel. Some lines of the novel causing world-wide uproar are worthwhile to recall here :

> "History the intoxicant, the creation...of the Devil ...against which the Imam has set his face. History is a deviation from the path, knowledge is delusion...the sum of knowledge was complete on the day Allah finished his revelation to Mohound."

And,

> "...and when Musa the grocer grumbled one day about the twelve wives of the prophet, The rule for him, another fox us.... The girls of the curtain — it

> was only by convention that they were referred to as 'girls' as the eldest was a woman well into her fifties, while the youngest, at fifteen, was more experienced than many fifty-years-old had grown fond of this shambling Baal,...they would tease him deliciously, flaunting their bodies before him, placing their breasts against his lips,...until Mohound mixed with his rule book the women dressed brightly, and all the talk was of fucking and money, money and sex, and just the talk, either." (pp. 379-80)

Some pilgrim places get their mirror-image in the novel. There is also a Jahilia, the city of sand; 'Tent of Black' stone called the curtain where twelve prostitutes who have given themselves the names of the twelve wives of Mohound in neighbouring Yathrib, Rushdie does not hesitate to name names, with the exception of the prophet. He has Hamza in the place of Mohound, Ayesha and others straight from the book. Moreover, the battles which the prophet had to win in order to convert people are very real. The other character like idol goddesses Lat and Mant are also part of Islamic folklore. The Hindu Gods are also subject to the satirical treatment in the novel :

> "After six movies playing the elephant headed god he was permitted to remove the...grey mask and put on instead, a long hairy tail in order to play Hanuman the monkey king in a sequence of adventure movies that owed more to a certain cheap television series emanating from Hong Kong than it did to the Ramayan. This series proved so popular that monkey tails become derigueur for the city's young bucks at the kind of parties frequented by convent girls known as 'firecrackers' because of their readiness to go off with a bang." (p. 24)

These lines were bound to trigger an avalanche of protest from the ramparts. Rushdie, though respected as writer of "uncommon talent" among educated elite, is regarded 'communal rabble rouser' or 'a motivated politician' by majority of the common folk.

Rushdie has realised fully the importance of historical facts in the fictional world. Except his first novel *Grimus* (1975), other two novels *Midnight's Children* (1980) and *Shame* (1983) are purely historical novels. In *Midnight's Children*, Rushdie's chief aim was to relate private life to public events and to explore the limits of individuality in a country as big, as populous and culturally variegated as India. Similar is the case of *Shame* for Pakistan to some extent. Rushdie is mainly involved in the most crucial events of the days in the United India. His subject matter is closely concerned with the politics of Indian sub-continent and his dealing and presentation of facts is really remarkable. He presents the most realistic historical facts under the influence of individual's actions and inspirations." The image of the writer, says Keith Wilson, "as both master and victim of public and private material, which he has been formed by in the present, dominates Midnight's Children." *Shame* is closely related to the politics in Pakistan and *Midnight's Children* is a novel about struggle of independence, the partition and their repercussions. The holocaust of partition of India has been presented in a realistic manner in the novel like Khushwant Singh's *A Train to Pakistan* (1956), B. Rajan's *The Dark Dancer* (1959), Manohar Malgoankar's *Distant Drum* (1969), Aattia Hussain's *Sunlight in a Broken Column* (1961) and Collins and Lapeirre in *Freedom at Midnight* (1975). With the help of Saleem's personal collective experiences, the novel virtually presents all the recent events of Indian history : the Jallianwalla Bag tragedy, Quit India Movement, Cabinet Mission, Struggle for independence, Muslim League and its role, communal riots and bloodshed, Five year plans, reorganisation of Indian states and language conflicts, Chinese aggression, the theft in Hazratbal Mosque, Pakistan war, liberation of Bangladesh, the Emergency and various other social and historical important events. There are the truthful pictures of typical Indian divisions and dissents, chaos and disillusion, communal tensions, religious fanaticism besides traditional values and modernizing efforts.

Moreover, Rushdie has used Indian historical events as a literary device to present and expose the human predicament in Indian society. He presents the common rhythm of life through the various aspects of Indian life. He sketches lively scenes, the absurdities, the pretensions, and the outer excitements and the traditional make up of the situations touched with his Indian historical events. His authentic descriptions are marked with intense realism. His characters, at the prime stage of life, are wonderfully innocent and show distinctive artistic presentations. Rushdie can cause to work as miracle using even a modest language resource with honesty and confidence. His themes, character, dialogues and straightforward statements are able to carry the feeling and atmosphere of Indian Society. He uses common Indian English idioms without bringing any change in their structure. His language is perfectly capable of presenting the ideas and suitable for amusement to the readers of east and west. He uses a lot of Indian words, *e.g.* Gunda, Chup, Amma, Takht etc. His vocabulary is large and adequate enough to deal with the range of subject matter. All these factors combined together have placed his name at the top among all the Indo-English novelists.

REFERENCES

1. Salman Rushdie, *Grimus* (Pan Books Limited, U.K., 1975).
2. Salman Rushdie, *Midnight's Children* (Pan Books Limited, U.K., 1980).
3. Salman Rushdie, *Shame* (Pan Books Limited, U.K., 1983).
4. Salman Rushdie, *The Satanic Verses* (Penguin Books Ltd., England, 1988).
5. Salman Rushdie, ''An Interview with Rushdie'', *The Mail* (June 18, 1983).
6. Dilip Fernanidez, ''How Good A Writer is Salman Rushdie?'', *Gentleman*, February, 1984.
7. Madhu Jain, ''An Irreverent Journey'', *India Today* (September 15, 1988).
8. David Devdas, ''Salman Rushdie : Political Scapegoat'', *India Today* : October 31, 1988.
9. David Devdas, ''On Rushdie, Art and Censorship'', *Times of India* : October 11, 1988.
10. R.S. Pathak, *Three Contemporary Novelist* : History and the Individual.
11. Roma Singh, *Midnight's Children : A critical study* (An M.A. dissertation; Patna University, 1986).

9

Novel As Indian Voice : A Study in Chaman Nahal

RAJESH KUMAR SINHA

Chaman Nahal, an essentially Indian writer, was born in the united India. He grew up in an Indian environment and culture. He opted English as the medium of his expression. Almost all his novels and short stories, however, mirror Indian life and problems. His characters bear Indian names, the setting of his novels is Indian and themes of his novels are Indian. To put it briefly, we get authentic depictions of the Indian ethos in his novels. "The Seatle Times" of U.S.A., with special reference to Nahal's *Azadi*, rightly comments;

> "Here is India. India colourfully,
> penetratingly, amusingly...
> No one but an Indian could have written his
> book and not many Indians would do it,
> as well as Chaman Nahal."[1]

When we go through the novels of Chaman Nahal, we realize that all his fictional work is truly Indian in spirit. But along with this realization a question also crops up in mind as to why Chaman Nahal has chosen to write in English and not in any other language. To answer this we may quote R. Parthasarathy who in his introduction to *The Twentieth Century Indian Poets*, rightly observes :

> "It is not surprising (therefore),
> that writers in English are
> conscious of their Indianness
> because, (at the bottom of it all),
> one suspects a crisis of identity."[2]

Chaman Nahal has substantially contributed to Indian English Fiction. Qualitatively, his novel belongs to high breed because each of them exudes different theme. One factor which is noticed in his novels, is the expression of Indian sensibility. It is this speciality of his novels that made him a novelist of international repute. His works have become popular because they embody Indian life, legend and philosophy. His attitude towards life is always positive as we find in his characters like Kamal, Kanshi Ram, Ravi and others. His fictions transmit a wholesome vision of life.

Nahal's vision has always been optimistic. His novels speak high of ethical and moral values. In his interview with B.S. Goyal (1984) he has expressed :

> I believe in an affirmation
> Of life in spite of all its odds
> And setbacks. Life is a series
> of crises until one emerges
> powerful and resplendent. I
> don't have commitment with
> a slant, I am only committed
> to the affirmation of life. Life
> consists in taking on the challenges
> and in the refusal to be beaten down.[3]

Indian legends have been frequently used by Chaman Nahal in his novel *My True Faces* (1973), the title itself has and linkage with vibhutiyoga (The Yoga of Divine Glories) enunciated in the 10th chapter of the Gita. In the light of the knowledge of the *Gita* the novelist has tried to educate that man should try to be one of his true faces, *i.e.*, true to him and true to Himself. The real Krishna of the Gita has been contrasted against the Krishna of popular imagination and myth.

Azadi (1975) is the masterpiece output of Chaman Nahal's artistic craftsmanship and creative genius. It is a shattering saga of the colossal tragedy and disruption that accompanied the partition and independence in the Indian subcontinent. Nahal is so much obsessed with the spirit of Indianness that he has given Hindi title to his English novel. Its protagonist Lala Kanshi Ram represents a typical Indian character.

The *Another Dawn* (1977) deals with the theme of universal love. Thematically speaking, this novel records the dichotomy of an Indian who finds himself hanging between the East and the West. Ravi, the hero of the novel, though marries an American woman named Irene in America but hardly finds himself settled there. When he suffers from terminal cancer he returns to his home Hardwar, the holy city of India, to die.

The English Queens (1979) is an attempt in an entirely new direction. This is the story of the six women "crowned" as the "Queens of the English Language." In fact, these queens are neither English nor really the queens of the language. This novel appears to be a crude satire on Indian's weakness for English Language.

The Crown and Loin Cloth (1981) is a record of the Indian's struggle for the freedom of the country. The very title is suggestive of the theme of the novel. This novel registers the confrontation between seemingly unequal forces between the mighty British Empire, *i.e.* "The crown" and the newly awakened India under the dynamic leadership of Mahatma Gandhi, *i.e.* the flimsy "Loin cloth."

Sunrise in Fiji (1988) deals with the theme of cross-culture which is already touched upon by the author in his novel into *Another Dawn*. Again the protagonist in this novel is an Indian architect known as Hariwansh. The story moves around him and ends with an optimistic note.

Thus, we see that novels of Chaman Nahal are pregnant with the spirit of Indianness. Theme may vary from novel to novel, yet the undercurrent is always Indian. Either the character is Indian or the philosophy is Indian or the legend is Indian. It can, therefore, be said that his novels genuinely tongue out the Indian voice.

REFERENCES

1. Chaman Nahal, *Azadi* (1988), Orient Paperbacks, New Delhi.
2. Hari Mohan Prasad, *Response : Recent Revelations of Indian Fiction In English* (1983), Prakash Book Depot, Bareilly.
3. M.K. Naik, *A History of Indian English Literature* (1885), Sahitya Academy, New Delhi.
4. R. Parthasarathy, *The Twentieth Century Indian Poets* (1991), Oxford University Press, New Delhi.

5. S.A. Mahazan,'' Chaman Nahal's *Azadi* : A socio pragmatic study''.

6. Singh, P.K., *The Novels of R.K. Narayan* : A critical evaluation (1999), Atlantic Publishers, New Delhi.

10

Thematic Complexity in Kamala Markandaya's *Nectar In A Sieve*

V.K. ARORA

The fictional world of Kamala Markandaya is thematically wide as her concern is social, economic, cultural and sometimes historical. Rural life, poverty, hunger, fear, despair and deaths are her recurrent themes. Her themes and concerns are typical. In *Nectar in a Sieve*, her concern is hunger and inner corruption that is anticipated through hunger. Dr. A.V. Krishna Rao considers it "the havoc of economics."[1] Rao observes, "In *Nectar in a Sieve*, Markandaya dramatises the tragedy of traditional Indian village and a peasant family assaulted by industrialisation. Rukmani and Nathan, the peasant couple in a south Indian village, are the victims of the two evils; zamindari system and the industrial economy."[2]

This is one of the ideas explicit in the novel which bears the social significance. But there are other inter-related themes. The basic issue is human existence in rural India that forms the subsidiary theme of the novel. On the other hand Kai Nicholson remarks : "In India, the countryside too has been polluted, but not by the encroachment of industry, for here it has not even shown its face. In the village the pollution comes from within : through starvation."[3] Dr. Rao explains that the happiness of Rukmani will soon disappear after the construction of the tannery. Everything appears to have happened in the 'twinkling of an eye'. The tannery, symbolical of mechanical power, finally destroys the traditional village. It brings inflation, vice and disease and completely disturbs the village life. Nathan "liked to see his sons beside him to teach them the ways of the earth how to sow, to transplant, to reap; to know the holesome from the rotten, the unwelcome read from the paddy." Now Nathan and Rukmani are waiting helplessly for the employment of their sons at the tannery. Sometimes rain and sometimes drought like condition upsets their life. Misfortunes come one after another. One of their sons is killed at the tannery. The crops fail. Another son dies of starvation. Their daughter, Ira takes to prostitution in order to live. The final assault is from the zamindar who tells them to vacate because they cannot pay him the rent. They go out to the town for seeking the help of their son but they return unable to find out his whereabout. Nathan dies of privation and disease. Tortured by man and nature Rukmani returns to her village to be with her son and daughter Ira. Rukmani herself paints a very tragic picture of hunger." Thereafter we fed on whatever we could find : the soft ripe fruit of the prickly pear, a sweet potato or two, blackened and half rotten, thrown away by some prosperous hand : sometimes a crab that Nathan managed to catch near the river. Early and late my sons roamed the countryside, returning with a few bamboo shoot a stick of sugarcane left in some deserted field, or a piece of coconut picked from the gutter in the town. For these they must have ranged widely, for other farmers and their families, in like plight to ourselves, were also out searching for food, and for every edible plant or root there was a struggle — a desperate competition that made enemies of friends and put an end to humanity. "She further explains that they were forced to eating grass to satisfy their hunger and how it feeds on man :" for hunger is a curious thing; at first it is with you all the time, waking and sleeping and in your dreams and your belly cries out insistently, and there is a gnawing and pain as is your very vitals were being devoured, and you must stop at any cost, and you buy a moment's respite even while you know, fear the sequel, then the pain is so longer sharp; but dull, and this too is with you always, so that you think of food many times a day and each time a terrible sickness assails you, and because you know this, you try to avoid the thought, but you cannot, it is with you." (p 87) these two pictures portray hunger very effectively and with pitiless realism. This presentation supplements the view that the dominant theme is that of hunger, starvation and death. There are also several other factors — zamindari system, Industrial economy tannery, exodus of Nathan, sons and vagaries of Nature and in some way or the other contributory to the uprooting of this family.

Nathan is a lease-holder and has to pay revenue for the use of land to his landlord in all circumstances. As the crops fail every year, Nathan is not in a position to pay the rent continuously for years, hence his landlord orders to evacuate the land. Moreover, his sons have no emotional involvement with the soil and they are not interested in their father's profession of tilling the land which does not belong to them. Furthermore, Nathan is evicted from his land which makes the matter worse. Now a landless Nathan is bewildered for livelihood which he earned as a leaseholder. Landlordism is also one of the themes in *Nectar in a Sieve.*

The vagaries of Nature also play a dominant role in *Nectar in a Sieve.* Starvation comes in Nathan's family when Nature goes against due to drought or excessive rain. Crop or no crop, Nathan has to live. It rains and rains and the paddy crops are washed away. Rukmani describes the vagaries of Nature. "It was as if nothing had ever been but rain, and the water pitilessly found every hole in the thatched roof to come in, dripping on to the already damp floor...but Nathan and I watched with heavy hearts while the waters rose and rose and the tender green of the paddy field sank under and was lost. (p. 39) The tragic vagaries of nature spoil the sweet harmony of a peasant's life. Rukmani says : "Nature is like a wild animal that you have trained to work for you. So long you are vigilant and walk warily with thought and care, so long will it give you its aid, but look away for an instant, be heedless or forgetful and it has you by your throat." (p. 40) She recalls : "It rained so hard, so long and so incessantly that the thought of a period of no rain provoked a mild wonder. It was as if nothing had ever been but rain..... (p. 38) Rukmani considers the tannery as the main cause of her family's tragedy, though she is never blind to the realities of life. She admits : "Tannery or, the land might have been taken from us. It had never belonged to us, we had never prospered to the extent where we could buy, and Nathan, himself the son of a landlessman, had inherited nothing and whatever extraneous influence the tannery may have exercised, the calamities of the land belong to it alone, born of wind and rain and weather, immensities not to be tampered by man or his creation. To those who live by the land there must always come time of hardship of fear and of hunger. (p. 78) Crushing between man and nature she explains her position : "Hope and fear. Twin forces that tugged at us first in one direction and then in another, and which one was stronger no one could say, of the latter we never spoke, but it was always with us. Fear, constant companion of the peasant. Hunger, ever at hand to jog his elbow should be relax. Despair, ready to engulf him should he falter, Fear; fear of the dark future; fear of the sharpness of hunger; fear of the blackness of death." (p. 79)

Though the hunger theme is a major concern of this novel, there is the theme of human degradation that hunger brings. The most beautiful Kunthi is driven by hunger to dubious ways of telling lies to her parents while to get a handful of rice. Raja moves in the compound of the tannery in search of something, may be to steal the costly hides. Ira cannot see Kunthi starving and she prostitutes with the workers of tannery. Money forces them for immoral trafficking, moral debasement and vice creep in on account of hunger. The novel appears to be mixed up with the theme of hunger and the theme of human degradation, but the former theme is much more forceful and effective. Hunger acquires epic dimension in this novel. The novel could not be touching if it is confined to an aspect, therefore, the novelist has provided it many dimensions, atleast thematically. The locale also remains not confined to a tiny village in South India, but it expands to whole of rural India.

Nectar in a Sieve is woven with numerous multicoloured threads running through its texture and the central thread is the rural society, the village of Nathan. It is being assaulted by the industrialisation establishment of a tannery. This tannery causes the decline of natural beauty. It plays havoc with village economy and uproots a tenant-farmer. It brings social degradation and loss of traditional values. Rukmani records the vast changes : "But the change that now came into my life, into all our lives, blasting its way into our village, seemed wrought in the twinkling of an eye." (p. 25) She compares past with present : "At one time there had been kingfishers here flashing between the young, shoots for our fish; and paddy birds; and sometimes, in the shallower reaches of the river, flamingoes, striding with ungainly precision among the water reeds, with plumage of a glory not of this earth. Now birds came no more, for the tannery lay close except crows and kites...." (p. 69) She is assertive and very critical of the tannery : "Some how I had always felt the tannery would eventually be out undoing I had known it since the day the carts had come with their loads of bricks and noisy dusty men, staining the clear soft greens that had once coloured our village and cleaving its cool silences with clamour. It had changed the face of our village beyond recognition and altered the lives of its inhabitants." (pp. 133-34) The industrialisation is really the root cause of the tragedy of Nathan's family. The tannery owners have purchased the land for their own extension. Thus, it is industrialisation that uproots the family from their village. Dr. A.V. Krishna Rao comes to the same conclusion when he says : "Nathan and Rukmani are representative of the thousands of uprooted peasants under an industrial economy."[4] Kamala Markandaya has, thus, presented a realistic picture of the impact of industrialisation of rural India. It might be considered one of its themes. Rukmani views this tannery as the source of all of her troubles : "None but these would have laid hands on her, even at her bidding. My sons had left because it frowned on them; one of them had been destroyed by its ruthlessness. And there were others its touch had scathed. Janki and her family the hapless Chakkli Kannan, Kunthi even.... (p. 134) An allied theme is given only a peripheral treatment or a passing mention. It is the theme of the destruction of the artisan's livelihood by the bigger organisation of industry. The tannery destroys the livelihood of a cobbler. Kannan Chakkli is infuriated by the order of the overseer to clear out from the maidan. He felt his livelihood wrested from the overseer. Previously he salted and tanned his own skins making them in to shoes and Chapals for the people of his people of his people. Now he realised that he has been driven out from his workshop.

There is yet another theme-tension between tradition and modernity. Tannery is the symbol of modernity and Rukmani's traditional village is on the otherside. This tension remains unresolved. Rukmani disapproves of the tannery time and again : "They may live in our midst but I can never accept them, for they lay their hands upon us and we are all turned from filling to barter and hoard our silver since we cannot spend it, see our children go without the food that they gorge." (p. 28) This theme is artistically assimilated in the plot, characterization and atmosphere of the novel. It is replete with overtones of sadness, pathos and tragedy of a joint Hindu family.

There is minor elaboration of the modern exodus as its theme. All the sons of Rukmani except Raja and Kunthi run away from land. Arjun and Thambi go to Ceylon and they never return. Murugan goes to the city and he is lost. His company of women and gamblers finally destroy him. This theme finds sketchy treatment, and elaborate treatment is in *A Handful of Rice*. Here we see Rukmani's son Murugan joining the exodus and leading a life of vice and filth in the city.

The East West encounter has also got sketchy treatment in this novel. We have one character Kenny, who is a humanist and representative of the finer tradition of the West. He helps Rukmani in many ways and is always a sympathiser to the family but Rukmani knows what Kenny is : "Have I not so much sense to see that you are not one of us? You live and work here, and there is in your heart solitude for us and love for our children. But this is not your country and we are not your people. If you lived here your whole life it still would not be." (p. 109)

A study of the major as well as minor themes in *Nectar in a Sieve* reveals that it is a novel of many multicoloured threads woven together and as such it has thematic complexity. We have a good number of themes both major and minor but the theme of hunger is most dominant. The themes are not complicated but they have been incorporated in a single story. The novel has no sub plot or side story. There is no intellectual substance but only traditional social milieu, the novelist is concerned with man's struggle with hunger. Rukmani's spiritual stamina, heroic impulse, dove-like simplicity, love of her children, tolerance and respect for traditional values make her an outstanding character.

REFERENCES

1. Dr. A.V. Krishna Rao, "Continuity and change in the novel of Kamala Markandaya's, *Perspectives on Kamala Markandaya's,* Vimal Prakashan, Ghaziabad, 1984, p. 4.
2. *Ibid*., p. 56.
3. Kai Nicholson, *Social problems in the Indo-Anglian and the Anglo-Indian Novel* (Bombay : Jaico Publication, 1972), p. 116.
4. Kamala Markandaya, *Nectar in A Sieve,* Hind Pocket Books. Subsequent references to the book are from this edition and page numbers are given in parentheses.

11

The Interaction of Individuality and Social Awareness in R.K. Narayan's Novels

PRAMOD KUMAR SINGH

R.K. Narayan's fiction forms the matrix of triumph for Indian creative literature in English. Narayan's fifty years of fiction writing earned him immense reputation both in India and abroad. The most fascinating feature of his personality is that he is a pure Indian both in thought and spirit despite his preference for English over his mother language for the expression of his creative urge. Living absorbed in religion and family, he is understandably indifferent to literary fashions of the west yet, he is almost a craze in the United States these days. Malgudi, the imaginary locale of his novels, is the panorama for the changing Indian Society. His fiction mirrors through his central-character the microcosmic India caught in the crucible of tradition and change.

"R.K. Narayan is the novelist of the individual man, just as Mulk Raj Anand is the novelist of the social man, and Raja Rao that of metaphysical man."[1] Narayan chooses a central-Character through whose view-point he looks at the various aspects of society as a silent on-looker. Mulk Raj Anand is a humanist and, therefore, to bring out human predicament is his prime concern. *Coolie* is a study of village-boy's sufferings who because of poverty is compelled to work as a servant. *Untouchable* introduces us the miserable condition of outcastes. *Two Leaves and a Bud* exposes the exploitation of the peasants by the Assam Tea Estate Owners. Anand's concern, therefore, is the economic exploitation and class distinction. The trilogy of *The Village, Across the Black Water* and *The Sword and the Sickle* is his sharp reaction against the traditional values of village society. *The Big Heart* presents an intimate picture of class and caste segmentation to which Anand himself belongs. *The Old Women and the Cow* depicts the pitiable condition of peasant in post-independence days. *Private Life of an Indian Prince* deals with the dying feudal system in India. We, therefore, see that Anand, like R.K. Narayan, is sharply aware of society and its all happenings. Yet, there is remarkable difference in between the two. Mulk Raj Anand looks angrily at the oddities and eccentricities of society but R.K. Narayan stares patiently and smiles.

Raja Rao is a metaphysical man. All his novels are charged with metaphysics. His *Kanthapura* presents the impact of Gandhian philosophy during the days of Non-cooperation Movement as well as the glory of Hindu mythology. *The Serpent and the Rope* presents symbolical difference between "illusion" and "reality" in Indian tradition. *The Cat and Shakespeare* deals with some middle class families of Kerala during the period of the Second World War. Raja Rao sees everything in the process of metaphysics 'yet' his novels are enriched with social consciousness.

R.K. Narayan is neither 'angry' like Mulk Raj Anand nor 'philosophical' like Raja Rao. Narayan's social consciousness is conspicuous in his novels yet his awareness is covered with a blanket of irony. He maintains a frontier of norms in his fictional writing and therefore, is free from all partialities. K.R.S. Iyengar explains how his artistic excellence is maintained under a nice limitation :

"He is one of the few writers in India who take their craft seriously, constantly striving to improve the instrument, pursuing with a sense of dedication what may often seem to be the mirage of technical perfection. There is a norm of excellence below which Narayan cannot possibly lower himself."[2]

Narayan minutely observes the society and presents most realistic pictures charged with gentle irony and light humour. His approach to subject-matter is always marked with intellectual inspirations. His artistic excellence lies in authentic exploration of fact in absolutely uninvolved matter.

R.K. Narayan's novels are teemed with social consciousness. "He is keenly aware of the fundamental irremediable incongruities which life and world are confronting with us."[3] He accepts the reality as it presents before him. He sees the society and its developments with an ironic detachment and accepts reality ungrudgingly. He sees no point in attempting to criticise or correct things because, as he remarks in *Mr. Sampath*, it seems to him "a futile and presumptuous occupation to analyse, criticise and attempt to set things right anywhere."[4] Narayan's central character shows us everything that occurs in every walk of society. R.S. Singh explains Narayan's art and object to fiction writing :

"Narayan's heroes are aware of social and political canvas, but they do not take sides, nor do they commit themselves any ideology. Narayan imbues them with social awareness and a sense of responsibility only to the extent it helps him to bring out their human qualities. His vision is comic and his central concern is vivid presentation of the ironies of life.[5]

He exposes the ills of society, and probes them too, but never for sadistic pleasure or for scatting disgust in readers. His chief aim is to highlight the hypocrisy of ideals, ambition and pride and not to guide the society in any particular direction but simply to make us realize.

Narayan's early novels are a sociological study of people's manners and mentality in pre-independence days. *Swami and Friends* (1935) highlights the existing manners as well as the impact of National Movement on common folk. *The Bachelor of Arts* (1937) is a probe into the every day incidents in a Hindu Household in South India and also the odd traditional norms of society. *The Dark Room* (1938) demonstrates the typical Indian attitude to family life and exposes the predicament of common house-wives. The heroine Savitri typifies all suffering house-wives of our society who are exploited by all means in their life. *The English Teacher* (1945) tells a tragic love story of the divine separation of two souls, with an alterior motif of satirizing the fault in existing education system which "makes us (nothing but) morons, cultural morons, but efficient clerks for all your business and administrative offices."[6]

The middle novels are Narayan's exploration into the manners and behaviour of people in post-independence era. The novels highlight the people's "modern desire for wealth."[7] *Mr. Sampath* (1949) is a story of a cunning rogue who without any corresponding ability wants to earn enormous wealth in very shortwhile. *The Financial Expert* (1952) "is an exact account of village usury and city deceit and a controlled probing into the motives of money making."[8] Both Sampath and Margayya represent the modern man who aspires to touch the sky in a jump and ultimately come back to the same old ground. *Waiting for the Mahatma* (1953) presents the socio-economic condition in the days of National Movement. It, moreover, highlights the impact of Mahatma Gandhi on the different strata of society. *The Guide* (1958), the most talked about novel, is appreciated for "depicting the ironies of modern Indian life."[9]

Narayan's metaphysical spirit is reflected from his later novels based mostly on Indian myths. We see that "the religious sense of Indian myth is part of Narayan's grim of reality, of his particular view of human life and his individual way of placing and ordering human feeling and experience. What one can say about Narayan without qualification is that he embodies the pure spirit of Hinduism."[10] Narayan is free from any partiality which lack in the case of Raja Rao in all of his mythical novels. *The Man-Eater of Malgudi* (1961) is based on the Hindu mythological legend of Bhasmasura. *The Vendor of Sweets* (1967) is based on the Hindu concepts of cyclical existence and four stages of human life. It simultaneously highlights the confrontation of tradition and modernity in Indian society. *The Painter of Signs* (1967) exploits with adroitness the story of ancient King Santhanu mentioned in *The Mahabharata*. The latest novel *A Tiger For Malgudi* (1983) is chiefly an exploration of philosophical Indian myths and metaphysical parables of Hindu religion.

Living absorbed in religion and family, Narayan is quite familiar with the developments within an Indian family. "The family is the immediate context in which his sensibility operates and novels are remarkably for subtlety and conviction with family relationship are treated."[11] He highlights the importance of a mother in *The Bachelor of Arts* and says, "mother is a sacred object. It is a commodity whose value we don't realise as long as it is with us" (p. 98). He realizes us that if Kailash had been a mother to look him after, he would have not been spoiled. Narayan, furthermore, believes that parents should deal firmly with their children because "only a battered son will grow into a sound man."[12] Mr. Sampath too thinks that "boys must be chastized, otherwise (they will) grow into devils" and hence he advises his son's tutor, any time you see him getting out of hand, don't wait for me. "Thrash him. Thrash him well...no boy who has not been thrashed has come to any good." Narayan expresses his dislike of dowry system and suggests the young celibates in *The Bachelor of Arts* that, "If one has to marry one must do it for love, if there is such a thing, or for the money and comforts. There is no sense in shutting your eyes to the reality of things." (p. 155)

Narayan is critical of caste system in Indian society. He makes us see that if Grace fears to come India, or Chandran to marry his sweetheart multicaste or class barrier happens to be the reason. Our society is ridden with caste and class feelings and hence when Jagan claims, "We don't believe in caste these days" or Raju says, "there is not caste or class today." We know pretty well how untrue they are. Narayan condemns caste or class division in almost every novel uninvolvedingly, yet in *The Bachelor of Arts* he fails to maintain his detachment and says, "If India was to attain salvation these watertight divisions must go — community, caste, sects, subsects, and still further divisions." He 'furthermore' dislikes the system of child-marriage and appreciates such "rational and modern people who abhorred the custom of rushing a young child into marriage." There is nothing in his work of the angry reform which informs the fiction of Mulk Raj Anand. Narayan's work contains no scalded sense of social injustice, no artificial anguish, no colonial indignation, and yet Narayan is clearly as Indian as any other Indian writer.

We, thus, arrive at the conclusion that Narayan is an unidentified social reformer, who is keenly aware of the various absurdities and eccentricities of society and suggests ironically the ways for their removal. It is, therefore, right to say that the story of Ram Gopal in *Mr. Sampath* is the story of Narayan's own who had almost "devoted his life to the abolition of the caste system and other evils of society." His ultimate ambition in life was to see his mother-land free from foreign domination. He was a disciple of Gandhi's philosophy, practising 'ahimsa' (non-violence) in though, word and deed. Narayan presents in his novels "Gandhi's pleas for non-violence with a new significance as one of the paths attaining harmony in life; non-violence in all matters, little or big, personal or national, it seemed to produce an unagitated, undisturbed calm, both in a personality and in society."

The intent behind this critical approach was to study the novels of R.K. Narayan assuming social consciousness on the nucleus of individuality. All his novels, from the simple sad comedy to the mythical nature, later parables are born in the smithy on social awareness. He is not an angry old man, nor a politician championing the cause of the masses. But he is a merchant of human metaphors, an artist with milk of human kindness flowing full in his heart. His fiction in its totality is an extensive metaphor on man at the centre of society.

REFERENCES

1. M.K. Naik, *The Ironic Vision*, Sterling Publisher Pvt. Ltd., Delhi, 1983.
2. K.R.S. Iyengar, *Indian Writing in English* : Asia Publishing House, Calcutta, 1973.
3. K.N. Sinha, *Indian Writing in English* : Heritage Publishers, New Delhi, 1979.
4. R.K. Narayan, *Mr. Sampath*, Indian Thought Publication, Mysore, 1973.
5. R.S. Singh, *Indian Novel in English,* Arnold-Heinemann, New Delhi, 1977.
6. R.K. Narayan, *The English Teacher*, Indian Thought Publication, Mysore, 1973.
7. William Walsh, *R.K. Narayan,* Allied Publisher Private Limited, New Delhi, 1983.
8. R.K. Narayan, *The Dark Room*, Orient Paperback, New Delhi.
9. R.K. Narayan, *Mr. Sampath,* Indian Thought Publication, Mysore, 1973.
10. R.K. Narayan, *The Vendor of Sweets,* Indian Thought Publication, Mysore, 1967.
11. R.K. Narayan, *The Guide*, Indian Thought Publication, Mysore, 1958.
12. R.K. Narayan, *The Bachelor of Arts*, Indian Thought Publication, Mysore, 1975.

12

Myth and Symbol in B. Rajan's *The Dark Dancer*

G. RAI

Balachandra Rajan is a well-known critic who has to his credit standard critical books on Eliot, Yeats and Milton. But as a creative writer he has been severely criticised. It is pointed out that Rajan has failed to understand Indian culture and tradition and the language he has used is artificial. V.Y. Kantak objects to Rajan's "mannered prose"[1] and according to Prema Nandkumar, "the main weakness of the novel lies in the uncertainty of its style."[2] David McCutchion points out that B. Rajan "has no gifts as a novelist" and *The Dark Dancer* reveals his "astonishing insensitivity to the language."[3] *The Dark Dancer* is a significant achievement in the post-independence Indian fiction. The use of myths and symbols in the novel has attained great artistic success. A close examination of these myths and symbols meets the charges of the critics that Rajan is unfamiliar with the country of his birth and that his language is artificial.

Myth has always been a literary device but in the recent times it has been employed to structure the chaotic modern condition in which traditional cultural values have disintegrated. The use of myth, as T.S. Eliot has pointed out, affords the artist both the necessary artistic control to explore his subject and the means of generalization. Myths are means to transmute personal destiny into the destiny of mankind. Northrop Frye observes that myth is expressive of the total vision of the human situation, human destiny, human aspirations and fears.[4]

Myth is an aesthetic means of expression of the complex interaction of the self and the world. G.S. Kirk points out that myth is a narrative with a dramatic structure and a climax and bears "important message about life in general and life within society in particular."[5] According to Rene Wellek myth is "the narrative or story, the archetypal or universal, the symbolic representation as events in time of our timeless ideals, the programmatic or eschatological, the mystic."[6] Ronald Barthes observes that "Myth has the task of giving an historical intention, a natural justification, and making contingency appear eternal."[7]

The central concern of the novel is the predicament in which the protagonist finds himself on his return to India after staying for ten years in a foreign country. Krishnan is in a state of dilemma. The problem that confronts him is that of identity the choice between two loyalties, the East and the West. He consents to the constrictions of an arranged marriage with the hope that it "would lead him to the precipice of belonging, the point of no return and no escape."[8] Cambridge is pursuing him in the seductive form of Cynthia. Krishnan temporarily forgets his desire for belonging and starts living with Cynthia when his Hindu wife Kamala is away from the scene so as to attend upon her ailing mother :

> He was happy with her because she only wanted him. There was no frame that he had to walk through for the fondness to come glowing into her face.... He was on an island, self, sustained and ringed by his contentment, but in front of him the continent lay, black desert, barren snow, jungle and village and the volcanic rocks of poverty, calling to him, inciting him, but no longer to be touched....(158)

Krishna would like to follow the ideals of Karna — "No one surpassed Karna in valour or skill of arms.... Even at the end he stayed unconquered." (133) Karna is one of those who fell victim to the inhuman cruelty of caste-system and rigid moral values. Karna was "the democratic man trying to be judged on his merits" (134) but society shut him out. He made his mistake the same way as Oedipus did and the retribution was greater than the flaw. But Karna is not the whole picture of Indian society. One must also remember Nanda who is a far better symbol of India — "He was a pariah. The priests wouldn't allow him even on the steps of the temple. But he prayed and prayed, and because of the strength of his devotion to God, the statue of Nandi, the great bull, moved aside, so that he could see the dancing image of Shiva." (134)

Krishnan is full of indignation against the Indian way of life in which man as an individual does not matter much. "Iron out the man for the convenience of the machine. If the system resulted in unreasonable consequences, blame the individual for getting in its way." (138) As a result of his Cambridge education and Western influence, Krishnan is attracted towards the superficial glamour of Western culture and is full of rebellion against the mystery and muddle of Indian culture because of moral degradation that has set in social life here. But he is not totally cut off from the cultural mores of India and his revolt is merely superficial. Moreover, he cannot stick to the West for ever because he lacks its emotional basis. By and large, he is dangling between two cultures. Rationally he is inclined towards the West while his emotions are curved to the pull of the East :

> He ought to rebel, but rebellion seemed inadequate when the forces opposing him were counterbalanced by the force within him that conformity claimed. A career arranged, a marriage predetermined. His private and public life inexorably charted. It should have shocked him and to some extent it did, but was the shock anything more than superficial, a tingle on the skin of his upbringing?.... He had the strange sense of detachment once again, of being both the dancer and the dance, of being the ritual and the ritual's object. (13-14)

The ideal of detachment in action preached to Arjuna, by Lord Krishna in the *Bhagavad Gita*, the disinterested action, *i.e.* doing one's duty without any thought for its fruit appears to be the ideal of Kamala's life. It is the source of her strength and inspiration in the critical moments of her life. Instead of trying to avoid disaster, a hope ridiculous in the age of Kali, she confronts it with dignity and in the appropriate manner. When abandoned by her husband, Kamala remains unperturbed :

> There was nothing in her voice, no bitterness, no resentment, not even curiosity about the manner of her defeat. She wasn't trying to reconvert the facts, to suggest that he might have misunderstood himself, to leave him a margin for his indecision, to hold out forgiveness as a bribe for change. (145)

Kamala is always true to her nature, consistent even in crisis. Her road is straight and clear, gently an assertion of her own self :

> She had let him go with an almost passionate reticence, never qualifying his freedom to choose by any appeal, or even by the shadow of any reproach. She had received him back with the happiness that was due to her, but not with bells ringing, with no apparent elation, or even satisfaction at a commitment rewarded.... She was uncompromising, a creature of the storm. (269)

She dedicates herself to the service of humanity and eventually lays down her life to save a Muslim prostitute. She is, by far, a symbol of a woman who wept and is quite appropriately equated with Draupadi and Damayanti who bore no malice for their husbands and took them back though their husbands had thrown "away their kingdoms at dice." (186) Reference is also made to "Sita's ordeal" (24) and it is suggested "that Kamala was the goddess Parvathi incarnate." (291)

The novel is set amid the turmoil and upheaval caused by the partition of the country and the widespread violence following it. Millions were uprooted and were faced with the problem of a choice as the country was divided between two nations :

> The award was the match that lit the long train of dynamite, shaking and ravaging across the chosen frontier.... And after the flaming sky and the broken bodies, after the wailing and the useless appeals, the striped flesh and the soliciting knees, raped, mutilated and torn into the silence, the exodus came, column upon column, blindly marching upon the vacant future, million upon million of the dispossessed in what seemed history's greatest tide of suffering. They

> had nothing to look for, only something to free from. (161)

The communal riot that disturbed the whole nation is related to the mythical wars of the West and the East — the battle of Troy and the battle of Kurukshetra, wars fought by the Greeks and the sons of Kunti respectively. "Homer's was a war of civilizations. The excuse was Helen's body, but they wanted the body of Troy. The sons of Kunti fought a war of fratricide. It was a war of annihilation to finally settle a gambling debt." (127)

The myth of incarnation, has for centuries exercised great influence on the life of the people of India who need God to steer their action. Whenever there prevails moral confusion and spiritual chaos and life is dominated by evil God incarnates himself to destroy immoral society and reestablish human values. God is related to man, this force gives man his dignity, it is also the source of his power. The worship of Lord Krishna has sunk deep into the heart and imagination of the people here. The novel is full of references to Krishna.

> In the centre of the storm the child lay naked, its ambiguous pose ready to kick and to welcome. He thought of Lord Krishna, the infant doomed by the tyrant king to death, carried into the safety of a different storm, into the welcoming of a different torrent.... One day, perhaps, it would grow up into justice, into the playing of mischievous music to milkmaids, one day into the captivating of the truth. (257)

The most powerful symbol that accounts for the structural unity of the novel is that of Nataraja. The novelist has given a very moving account of the dance of Shiva :

> He saw the great figure of the Nataraja, one leg arched in that supreme expression of energy, the dying smile of the demon beneath the other's lightness, all that infinite power of destruction drawn back into the bronze circle of repose — ''Neither flesh nor fleshless 'Neither from nor towards', at the still point there the dance is." Paradox, contradiction,

> miracle — they were the barriers to which explanation was driven. But at least in that hypnotic figure the paradox was a radiance in one's senses the intense union of power with tranquillity, not captured but liberated in that eternal dancing. (28)

The cosmic dance of Shiva symbolizes both creation and destruction as antithetical yet complementary forces. Its aesthetic and emotional associations have deep-roots for the people of India — "(Shiva) is the soul of all, and his dance is the creation preservation, and destruction of the universe, and the giving of bodies to souls and their release. The dance is ceaseless and eternal. Ati Sheshan shall behold it again at Tillai, Chitambaram, the centre of the universe."[9] The symbol of *Nataraja* is fully integrated with the thematic content of the novel and the arguments of K.R. Srinivasa Iyengar that Symbolism has no "clarity and force"[10] and Harimohan Prasad that Rajan's images "buckle under their own load"[11] are unacceptable. Krishnan is deeply moved to hear the song about Nataraja and on his return to Kamala at Shantipur he is attracted to the same image and relates the widespread violence to the trampled foot of Shiva — "one is aware of the shadow, of the dancer's leap clanging in every disaster" (267). The Nataraja's repose within the circle of flames brings out effectively the cyclic relationship of the dance of death with the dance of life. He becomes aware of the importance of detachment and right action for its own sake and finds solace in the words of Krishna to Arjuna :

> He who seeks freedom,
> Thrusts fear aside,
> Thrusts a side anger
> And puts off desire
> Truly that man
> Is made free for ever. (312)

The country also undergoes a traumatic experience. She experiences death and destruction but shall rise again to a new birth and reconstruction. Thus the myths and symbols help the novelist to portray the present in parallel to the past. This method stresses the basic fact that the present phenomenon is only a recurring problem of human history.

Thus the novel is full of references to the events and characters of the past which have been used in literature as myths. Krishna is 'the son of Kunti — Arjuna in his indecision and evasion from killing, and Karna in his problem of finding his true identity. The main theme of the novel is that of a man trying to find himself. This is what Karna and Arjuna both are doing in *Mahabharata* against the holocaust of events. The names Krishnan a variation of Lord Krishna or Vishnu and Kamala, a variation of Lakshami are really a suggestion that in these days people like these are the 'avatars' of goodness and virtue. Some of the myths are underlaying the novel and bring out its meaning. But quite a few help in the understanding of the characters, their essential meanings, situations and dilemmas. All these myths place the present and the local as but a point in the continuity of times and the vastness of the world. The method of portraying the present in relation to the past adds a new dimension. The newness of one situation is but a variation upon what has happened in various climes and times. These are archetypes of historical events and of characters which are repeated again and again. This emphasises the universality and eternity of the issues raised in the novel and prevent its theme from becoming journalistic.

NOTES AND REFERENCES

1. Quoted by H.S. Saxena, "Balachandra Rajan" in *Essays in Criticism : Indian Fiction in English*, ed. O.P. Bhatnagar (Jaipur : Rachana Prakashan, 1980), p. 30.
2. *Ibid.*, p. 30.
3. *Ibid.*, p. 30.
4. Northrop Frye, *Anatomy of Criticism : Four Essays* (New Jersey : Princeton University Press, 1957, 1971), p. 136.
5. G.S. Kirk, *The Nature of Greek Myths* (Penguin Books, 1974), pp. 28-29.
6. Rene Wellek and Austin Warren, *Theory of Literature* (1942, Penguin Books, 1968), p. 191.
7. Ronald Barthes, *Mythologies*, trans. Annette Lavers (New York : Hill and Wang, 1952, 1972), p. 142.
8. Balachandra Rajan, *The Dark Dancer* (London : William Heinemann Ltd., 1959), p. 19. All subsequent references are to this edition and are indicated by page number in the parenthesis.
9. Nivedita and Coomaraswamy, *Myths of the Hindus and Buddhists* (London : George G. Harrap & Company Ltd., 1918), p. 312.

10. K.R. Srinivasa Iyengar, *Indian Writing in English* (1962, New Delhi : Sterling Publishers Pvt. Ltd., 1985), p. 509.
11. Hari Mohan Prasad, "Theme of Exile in Indo-English Novel in *Alien Voice : Perspectives On Commonwealth Literature* ed. A.K. Srivastava [Lucknow : Print House (India), 1981], p. 212.

13

Arundhati Roy's *The God of Small Things* : A Mirror of Contemporary Indian Psyche

PRAMOD KUMAR SINGH

Arundhati Roy, after receiving the 1997 Booker Prize for her first novel *The God of Small Things*, has earned a place among the contemporary literary jewels of the world like Amitav Ghosh, Shobha De, Salman Rushdie, Bharti Mukherjee, V.S. Naipaul, Vikram Seth, Rohinton Mistry and Vikram Chandra. This prestigious award to the novel, apart from being a tribute to the literary excellence of Arundhati, is an acknowledgement of the ascendancy enjoyed by Indian Writing in English on the international scene of world's literature. In the novel *The God of Small Things,* with its plot set in a woodsy Kerala hamlet, the novelist has universalized 'Ayemenam' in the manner of R.K. Narayan's *Malgudi* and Gabriel Gracia Marquez's *Macondo.*

The novel presents vivid and lively pictures of South Indian society, particularly of the villages and sub-urban areas of Kerala. The pictures are so alive that the readers sometimes feel as if the history of South India has been redrawn before them. Describing the novel, Prof. Gillian Beer, the Chairman of the Booker panel of Judges, said that Arundhati Roy funnelled the "history of South India with extraordinary linguistic inventiveness. The story she tells is fundamental as well as local. It is about love and death; about lies and laws. Her narrative crackles with riddles and yet feels its tale quite clearly. We are all engrossed by this moving novels."[1]

The novel has been criticised by host of critics and politicians for being dubbed as a satire on the politics of communist party and its leaders. The Chief Minister of Kerala E.K. Nayanar, who had earlier congratulated Arundhati on her winning the Booker Prize since he was a Malayalee and the daughter of a communist activist Mary Roy, later criticised the novel by saying that the only notable thing about her book *The God of Small Things* was the "anti-communist poison"[2] in it. Nayanar said that the west was praising the book probably because of its anti-communist tone. He further remarked that the Booker prize was earlier given to V.S. Naipaul also who had vilified the leaders of India in his book.

The story of novel moves around its central characters, Ammu, her son Estha and daughter Rahel. The sad plight of Ammu, a prostitute, throws light on the inhuman treatment bestow upon the prostitutes of Ayemenem in Kerala. The policemen approach the 'Veshyas' (prostitutes) with snicking scissor in order to hack off their heirs. Ammu often painfully noticed in the market of Kottayam many helpless women with vacant eyes and being forcibly shaved by policemen. This was the reason that Ammu prefers to die unnoticed and lonely in a grimy room of Bharat lodge in Alleppey where she had gone for a job interview.

The novel throws light on the political activities of communists in Kerala. The naxalites fight to ensure payment of minimum wages to the labourers as specified by the Trade Unions. The Naxalites also consciously fought against the sexual exploitation of poor and helpless women by their employer and forced men from good families to marry servant girls whom they had made pregnant in the course of their employment. The novel satirizes the politician, who do politics of vested interest and throws light on such politicians often doing politics for serving their own interests in the garb of serving people through their political activities. This was the reason that the communist leader K.N.M. Pillai never came heavily against his political rival Mr. Chacko because of his own private business relating printing of pickles labels by his printing press for which orders were obtained with the help of the rival leader.

The element of sex and sensuousness are ample in the novel. In Chapter VIII, Mammach wanted to examine the bedsheet for stains in order to find out the sexual relationship between Margaret Kochamma with Chacko. In Chapter I, the Police Inspector Thomas Mathew lustfully eye at the breast of Ammu and tap it by his baton.

The 'veshyas' at Kottayam are so deprived of human rights that the Inspector do not prefer to take statement of a prostitute and their illegitimate children as a witness;

> "He started at Ammu's breast as he spoke. He said the police knew all they needed to know and that the Kottayam police did not take statement from veshyas or their illegitimate children. Ammu said she'd see about that. Inspector Thomas Mathew came around his desk and approached Ammu with his baton."[3] (p. 8)

The conversion of Dalits into Christianity and the feeling of untouchability is one of the prime concern of the novelist. After arrival of Britishers to Malabar, a large number of people from Paravans, Pelayas and Pulayas castes were converted into Christianity and joined the Anglican church to escape the scourage of untouchability. For accepting conversion, they were given a little food and money by the missionary and hence other people called them as "Rice-christians." The converts soon realised that they have jumped from the frying pan into the fire. They were segregated from other Christians having separate churches, services and separate priest. After independence, they found, they were not entitled to any Government facilities for scheduled castes like job reservations or bank loans at low concessional rates because officially now they were Christians and, therefore, belong to a casteless community. For being an untouchable, Vellya Paapen was send to the school of untouchables founded by Punnyan the father-in-law of Mammachi.

When Mammachi hired the service of Velutha, a Parayan for carpentry works of her factory, it caused a great deal of resentment among the other touchables factory workers because they thought that the Paravans are not meant to work as carpenters. In order to appease resentment of other touchable workers, Mammachi pays less wages to Velutha.

> "To keep the others happy, and since she knew that nobody else would hire him as a carpenter, Mammachi paid Valutha less than she would a touchable carpenter but more than she would a Paravan. Mammachi did not encourage him to enter the house

> (except when she needed something mended or installed). She thought that he ought to be grateful that he was allowed on the factory premises at all, and allowed to touch things that Touchables touched."[4] (p. 77)

Arundhati is a pure Indian both in thought and spirit. So it was really a feat for her to achieve a success of functional writing in an alien language. She views socio-political situations of South India with an ironic detachment yet highlights almost each and every incident happening around her which an ordinary eye is prone to miss. She appears supremely sensitive to the various social evils such as untouchability, involuntary conversion of religion, abuse of official positions by politicians and police, deprivation of human rights to sexworkers and dalits, adultery and host of others. Her characters are ardently aware of political hypocrisy of communist leaders of Kerala. They act and react with various incidents of society and give minute historical details of immediate post-independence situation of South Indian society. Arundhati uses gentle irony and simple words for expression of her creative urge of fictional writing. Probably this technique has enabled her to achieve the supreme success in fictional writing. The mental agony of Ammu is not of her alone but represents whole of the suffering women (prostitutes) of South India. The story of communist leader K.N.M. Pillai is not a story of his own and in fact it tells tale of political hypocrisy, snobbery and treachery of whole lot of politicians in Kerala.

REFERENCES

1. Modi, Anjali, *Indian Express*, Oct. 15, 1997 : "Amma Roy....this is calling to tell."
2. *Indian Express*, Oct. 31, 1997 : "Nayanar spews Venom on Roy Book."
3. Roy, Arundhati, *The God of Small Things* (India Ink Publishing Co. Pvt. Ltd., New Delhi), 1997. All references are to this edition and are indicated by page number in the parenthesis.
4. *Ibid*.
5. Menon, Leela, *Indian Express*, Oct. 25, 1997 : "Ayemenem Revisited."
6. Menon Sreelatha, *Indian Express*, Oct. 10, 1997, "Small Things bother Them."

14

The Concept of New-Woman in Shashi Deshpande's Novel : *That Long Silence*

PRAMOD KUMAR SINGH AND R.K. GUPTA

Shashi Deshpande, a prominent and up-coming Indo-Anglian writer, has delineated the undulations of the female ego or self under the pressure of critical human predicaments and emotional affinities. Her attention is focused on feminine sufferings in Indian society. The feminist literary tradition is grown out of the anxieties of woman's life. The very basis of feminism is reformist. The fundamental reality of woman's life situation, its "interrupted" nature, perhaps is the reason for a close connection between woman and fiction writing. Mostly, definitions about women's conduct, behaviour and existence were given by men. The old conventional notions of male dominated society were so rude, unbearable, suppressive, oppressive and depressive that women's discourse takes a shape of movement. Their consciousness seeks to analyse and understand the material conditions through which gender has been constructed within specific languages and bodies of literature. And its outcome is that the strong wave of new-women in 1960s and 1970s took a place for women's liberations.

The concept of new-woman will have justified itself only by bringing about a radical change in public attitude towards man-woman relationships. The general perspectives about woman as a shadow-figure to a male caretaker, be he a father, a husband or a son, continue to persist. Man's affinity with woman is most often the bond that exists between a master and a slave. This state calls for a concerted effort to demolish such notions and to assert the dignity and equality of woman in the family as well as in the wider social life.

Shashi Deshpande's novels reveal the women's quest for self, an exploration into the female psyche and an awareness of the mysteries of life and the protagonists' place in it. Her first novel *Roots and Shadows* published after *The Dark Holds No Terrors* and *If I Die Today*, and all these novels indicate the initial quest of women for herself. The same quest is continued in her later novel *That Long Silence*. The novelist explains that all her protagonists are related with their "selves". Her women, like those of her predecessor, are tolerant, obedient, passive and submissive. But the concept of new-woman is all along markable in their feelings and conducts. The title of the novel *That Long Silence* suggests a belated reaction, postponement of offensive behaviour for long till postponement cannot be made any more. The patience of silence and endurance is broken and its outcome is a new-woman with egotistical affirmations and emotional explosions. As Shashi Deshpande herself states : "Innermost feelings come out in my writings. The kind of emotions we know women have but never come out."[1]

In the novel *That Long Silence* Mrs. Deshpande depicts the anxiety and difficulty of a middle class family. Mohan, to obtain name and fame as well as prestige and security, is involved in some maldeeds as a result of which he faces inquiry and loses his job. Agarwal, a co-partner in the same deeds advises him to stay away from the office until the storm is over. Mohan, alongwith his wife, Jaya, decides to go and reside for a while at Jaya's maternal uncle's flat in Dadar. They lived there till the shifting to a big flat in Churchgate. Although in silent indignation, the mode of self-examination and self-criticism begin for Jaya. As she makes excuses (it was all Appa's fault. Why had he made me feel I was someone special?" 138) to the realization that "in releasing them from the slats I'd put them in I've released myself somehow." (180) She is ever haunted by the memories of the past — her earlier life and her marriage with Mohan. The desperations and disappointments in her seventeen years old marital existence, her personal failures, all these begin to haunt and torment her. Jaya can no longer be a passive, submissive and silent partner to Mohan. The novel ends with her determination to speak, to break her long silence. This way she is representative of girls who are brought up in middle-class families in post-Independent India.

That Long Silence depicts Jaya's self-doubts, fears, guilt, silent indignation towards articulation and assertion. Suman Ahuja, a reputed critic, observes that Jaya "Caught in an emotional eddy, endeavours to come to terms with her protean roles, while trying albeit in vain, to re-discover her true self, which is but an ephemera....an unfulfilled wife, a disappointed mother and a failed writer."[2]

The novelist is not only writing about her female protagonist, Jaya, who is trying to remove a long silence and struggle with the problems of self-revelation and self-estimation, but, through Jaya, also about other women, those unhappy preys who never broke their silence. For example, at one place in the novel, Jaya realizes that her name is not figured in the family tree. When Jaya asks her uncle, Ramukaka, why her name is not included in the family tree, she is given to understand that she now belongs to her husband's family and not to her father's. But this is not quite true. Neither her mother nor her Kakis (uncle's wife), not even her ajji (grandmother) that indomitable woman, "Who single-handedly kept the family together" (143) find a place in the family tree. Jaya feels that her name and existence, alongwith those of other women in the family, are fully effaced from the list of family history. Jaya's protest against such kind of order which is given to women in our culture depicts another vision from women's point of view.

The novel presents a scathing aspect of our social institutions like marriage or family. For instance, during her pregnancy, when Jaya advises Mohan that he should do the cooking, Mohan is highly amused by this advice and thinks that cooking is not a man's business. But the sight of Kamat doing the cooking made her uneasy. Kamat is Jaya's up-stairs neighbour at Dadar. He is a widower and his only son has settled abroad. He lives alone in the house and hence he performs his all deeds without any one's help. Here we find Jaya's relationship with Kamat. Kamat has shown a lot of understanding and sympathy for Jaya. Jaya, too, is more free with him than she is with her husband. But such type of friendship between a married woman and another man is always looked down upon. That is why when Kamat's dead body was lying on the floor of his flat Jaya did not stay and pay homage to her best friend for the fear of destroying her wedding. So she does her role of a wife but fails as a human being. She belies for a while the loyal Hindu ideal of devotion to husband. Her romantic appearance is the feminist mark of the new-woman. But after all she concludes that a husband is a "sheltering tree" and she plays again the role of an orthodox Hindu wife. There can be no life without her husband, Mohan. His telegram confirms that he is coming. But life with Mohan now must be put on a new footing : "If Mohan returns, I thought if only Rahul and Rati came back, we can begin living afresh" (182).

The concept of Jaya's ego becomes evident when we consider the husband-wife relationships of the traditional Hindu women and the new-women. Jaya's mother never raised a voice against her father. Mohan thinks Jaya is not sufficiently trained to play the role of a good wife. "Her mother did not prepare her for the duties of a woman's life" (83). So a woman in anger is "ugly and unwomanly." (83) The novelist through Jaya-Mohan affinity has shed some light on modern love, sex, marital affinities and has hinted at the domestic warfare of married couples.

Jaya is symptomatic of the emerging new-woman. She has already developed a maxim that the daughter must fight the mother if she wants to graduate in the world. In keeping with this view she marries Mohan, because she finds that her mother is opposed to this match. Her maid-servant Jeeja plays an important part in her understanding of life's equation with mundane reality. The novelist presents some elements of new-woman in the novel *That Long Silence*. The pre-matrimonial love of Jaya and Mohan is a good paradigm of new-woman. Mohan was enamoured of Jaya's modernity and her modern education. With a new feminist frankness Jaya presents inter-dependence of love and sex : "First there's love then there's sex — that was how I had always imagined it to be. But after living with Mohan I had realised that it could so easily be the other way round." (95) Woman's realisation between of her solitude in the "act of sex" (98) and the possibility of love without bodily union (157) (as in the case of the affinity between Jaya and Kamat) are delineated clearly and add an unorthodox frankness to an abstruse awareness.

Jaya, as a wife and a mother, has done no justice to her own talents. Years back Jaya begins as a writer by producing a story which has won the first prize and is published in a magazine. But her husband, Mohan, assumes that the story is about their personal life. So Mohan under the pressure of his suspension and social complications arising from it and nervous irritations caused by humiliation and the need of hiding facts from family and friends, accuses Jaya of changed behaviour in the days of adversity. The undesirable accusation puts her into anger and insanity and she giggles violently and angrily on Mohan's accusations : "I had to control myself, I had to cork in this laughter. But it was too late. I could not held it any longer. Laughter burst out of me, spilled over, and Mohan stared at me in horror as I rocked helplessly." (122) This incident affects her career as a writer and it has left a deep impression on her psyche. Besides it, she has continued to write under an assumed name (as women writers have often done under patriarchy) but her stories has been rejected. Kamat comes to her help and reproves her : "I'm warning you — beware of this 'women are the victims' theory of yours. It'll drag you down into a soft, squashy bag of self-pity. Take yourself seriously, woman. Don't skulk behind a false name. And work — work if you want others to take you seriously." (148) Here Kamat appeared as a hard critic. He points out that the basic truth of her failure is her fear. In her failure Jaya is weak woman; in her failure she is a new-woman, who is weaker than the traditional woman of Indian ethos. Shashi Deshpande presents a new concept of feminist element in this novel.

Jaya, taking no such hard criticism, has resumed her career as a wife, as a mother. In the meantime Mohan has advised that she should write light, humorous pieces in the newspapers, what they called "middles". Jaya has then started her weekly column "Seeta" which has won the approval of the readers, the editors and above all of her husband. And for Jaya, as she observes, "she had been the means through which I had shut the door, firmly, on all those other women who had invaded my being, screaming for attention : women I had known I could not write about, because they might — it was just possible — resemble Mohan's mother or aunt or my mother or aunt." (149) Jaya is not free to act at will; she is a slave of her emotional affiliations and under limited conditions only she can follow the theory of "Yathechchhasi tatha Kuru" — Do as you desire, as Lord Krishna giving the message of 'Karma' to Arjuna on the battlefield, "I have given you the knowledge. Now you make the choice." (192) This way Jaya's self as a writer that is being crushed and this leads her to a rebellion. She herself delineates how she gave up writing for the joy of wifehood and motherhood : "Even a worm has a hole it can crawl into. I had mine — as Mohan's wife, as Rahul's and Rati's mother...and so I had stopped writing." (148) The situation in the narrative of *That Long Silence* arrives when, Jaya, its protagonist, is almost on the breaking point. The novelist has tried to clarify that under patriarchy women have also recoiled from telling the truth about their sex and self.

There has been a revolutionary and egocentric note in Jaya's character right from her early stage. Her father loved the classical music of Polushkar and Faiyaz and recommended it to Jaya, but Jaya was fond of the lilting music of Rafi and Lata. (3) Jaya's reaction to her own father speaks of her temperamental nature. The feminist rebellion and defiance, epitomised in Jaya's conduct, are based on the balance of the desertion of bad and acceptance of good in the time — honoured values and traditions. Jaya, like most of her new-woman, wants, only mundane joys, security and family harmony. The novelist presents an optimistic view through these words of Jaya : "We have to go on trying."[3] One has to believe in one's self; Jaya will begin life a new, for life provides many choices." (198) This is the sapience Jaya has learnt in the turmoils of her life. She has an opportunity in her life to act according to her choice.

Thus, as the title of the novel indicates, Jaya, for her seventeen years past life, has tried to play the role of a traditional woman, the embodiment of tolerance, suffering and courage. However, she becomes the modern egotistical self-assertive rebellious woman — all these being marks of new-woman. The desertion of the conventional passive and submissive role and adoption of the new role present a woman's perspective on the world and it focuses on women's issues.

NOTES

1. Shekhar, Ratna Rao, "Shashi Deshpande : That Long Silence Breaks", *Society*, Bombay, Dec. 1989.
2. Ahuja, Suman, ''Review'' in 'The Times of India', 8th October, 1989, p. 2.
3. Iyengar, K.R.S., "Indian Writing in English", Sterling Publishers, New Delhi, 1985, p. 758.

15

The Blue Bedspread : Twisted Autobiography of An Alienated Man

KRISHNA KANT SINGH

Raj Kamal Jha's *The Blue Bedspread*, although his very first novel, presents his depth and profundity of imagination which explores and points some of the untraditional and unorthodox human experiences. In this novel, Raj Kamal Jha narrates the hopes and aspiration on the one hand, and dejection and frustration on the other hand through the hero's confessions. In the novel that is breath-taking, solid and precise, the novelist discovers love and hope behind the hidden violence and twisted eroticism of an old city, Calcutta, a city of culture and tradition. It is the profoundly moving story of the lower middle class people who, through their imagination, find the escape they so desperately seek, but unable to come out from biding the truth for a desired longer period.

In *The Blue Bedspread*, Raj Kamal Jha has faithfully but ironically depicted the importance of family relationship as it always happens to one of main themes of the leading Indian novelists. In this novel, the chapters entitled like "Father', 'Mother', 'Brother', 'Sister', and 'Visitors' present his attitude towards the important aspects of human relationship which is shaken by modern implications in the modern era. The hero of the novel (whose name is not given) wants to fulfils his aspirations through these human relationship. All the important ingredients of human relationship — father, mother, sister, brother and visitors are treated in this novel ironically. The hero of the novel suffers a lot because, as the rule of human existence, his father, mother, sister and the visitors leave him alone to face the reality of human existence.

Raj Kamal Jha has adopted a complex and flash-back method to express the leanings and longings of his characters. The hero starts his presentation after receiving the phonecall of his sister's death. He tells the sad and painful stories of his life to the newly-born baby of his daughter. He now is not able to hide the facts in his heart for a longer period because after the death of his sister, his life has become meaningless. There is no one to accompany him except three days old baby. His feeling of alienation and boredom can be noticed by his confessions :

> I am not a young man any more.
> I wear glasses, my stomach droops
> over the belt of my trousers.[1]

In this novel, the hero tells the stories of his life in confessional manner, but in contemplative mood. Many times, he twisted facts to ironize them. His emotional attachment with the newly-born baby compel him to go back about his life. He speculates over his father, mother, sister and some other relatives who are no more. His father is a typical Indian father who is always conscious about the welfare of his children and does not allow them to engage in eating, drinking and merry-making. Being belonged to lower-middle class, he does not have enough money to spend on them. He does not allow them to flower according to their own will and likings. Sometimes, the brother and the sister feel themselves inferior to their class-mates come to school by motor-car. In the lunch time, they are not able to buy ice-creams because they have no enough money for entertainment. Their economic condition is so miserable that they taste ice-creams only once in a week. His geniusness and his sister's incomparable beauty attracted many students and they give them ice-creams frequently :

> There are students in my class who do not have to wait for five days, who eat ice-creams everyday, expensive ice-creams, the kind which comes in biscuit-cones or plastic-cones or plastic cups. They are rich students but because I come first in class and because my sister is very beautiful they all come

> to me for help before the examination. May be that is why I do not feel so bad.[2]

The role of the father is extremely important in the novel. Raj Kamal Jha has beautifully presented the effect of inferiority complex on the growing children through 'one rupee episode'. One day, when they return from the school, their father demands the change. His sister gives all the coins, but the coin of one rupee is missing. The one rupee coin is in Brother's pocket because it is he, and not the sister, who has collected the change from the bus-conductor. His father beats his sister cruelly for which she is not responsible. He does not dare to tell his father about the truth :

> Father is so angry and I am so scared that I cannot tell him all this now. Not once does sister tell him that it was I who got the change from the conductor today, she remembers everything by heart, she does not remember I could have made a mistake.[3]

The hero of the novel always feels loneliness and alienation which is the central theme of the novel. While describing the features of his shrewd father, he sometime hovers around past and present, because present is not brighter than the past. The father is always busy in drinking and beating his mother, he speculates over his future which seems to be futile for him. Raj Kamal Jha paints the alienation and boredom of the hero :

> During the night, the man gets up to check on the baby, to see why it is silent, why it is crying.... And while he is doing all this, the city keeps watching him, irritated and angry. In just a few hours, the darkest of the night, the foundations of their friendship will crack, the pillars of his solitude, the walls, will begin to buckle, some will even give way. The night will grow darker, the city, once spurned, will begin searching for another lonely man, or woman in the some other neighbourhood.[4]

In the chapter entitled 'Sister' Raj Kamal Jha has presented some unorthodox implications which are influencing human beings to surrender themselves against alienation, frustration and gloominess. Even though the novelist reaches the climax in the last pages of the novel, but here he has manifested an entirely uncommon and improper kind of human relationship which is not seen in Raj Kamal Jha's predecessor's novels. The hero of the novel unfolds the truth dramatically to the new born three days old baby. He is telling the entire story before her who seems to be the unwanted representative of his sister. On the contrary of the traditional values and conventional feeling, he does not hesitate to present an erotic picture of his sister :

> Today, she has used both; her hair, black and smooth, falls over her shoulders. Her lips are red, she wears a blue skirt and a white top with tiny blue stars.
>
> Sister never looked so beautiful.[5]

The Blue Bedspread is an ample manifestation of modern man's disillusionment where the traditional and the conventional concepts of relationship and living together have been replaced by immorality and strong desire to rush towards violent method to shock the common and prevalent by uncommon and rare. The relationship between the brother and the sister is pious and holy right from the beginning. They eat together, go to school daily in the same bus, take lunch in the internal jointly, came to home again in the same bus, share music, experiences, and cruelty of the father together, bear the harsh responsibilities of home in common, and even sleep on the blue bedspread together. Their everything is common and this is the great comfort for them. He (brother) says :

> "Father's gone, Babhani is gone, I am so tall that the wash-basin comes to my waist. Sister's hair is still black and beautiful, the iron hook is still there but the cage is gone, the birds where I don't know, your mother and I are leaning against the bedroom door, her left hand is on the binge, her right is in mine, norwester blows but the rain has stopped, the smell of wet earth and the wind run their fingers through her hair.... It is like in happy stories and movies, the neighbourhood is as pretty as it should be when a brother and a sister meet, for one day and half a night, in fifteen years."[6]

The brother faithfully reveals his relationship with his beloved. In the chapter entitled 'All Alone', Raj Kamal Jha has depicted the modern implications of horror, love, sex, and passion which have considered as the essential parts of human existence in modern era. The hero and his beloved go to Cinema for entertainment, but their entertainment in the farm of 'passion' goes beyond moral bias and piousness of their relationship. In the Cinema hall, the hero and his beloved begin to respond their amorous longings :

> She always wears a skirt on our Cinema nights. To let me slip my left hand between her legs. No unbuttoning of buttons, no noise of zips being unzipped. Nobody wears her skirt ride over her knees; she is dark, I'm dark, the Cinema hall is dark and nobody notices my left hand press her right knees.[7]

The hero and his beloved are in erotic mood and they are not able to suppress their passions. She is not aware of the importance of chastity. Like T.S. Eliot's typist girl, she is ready to surrender herself before his amorous advances. It is a typical influence of distorted modernity which is becoming quite normal and welcoming in these days. There is no role of sex and passion between man and woman before marriage, and it is sin and unholy for a man to concentratehis eyes on a woman. The inter-actions, advances and mutualresponses of the hero and his beloved are not mere notions to fulfil erotic desires, but it is a violent attack on Indian traditional outlook of love :

> I slide my fingers deep, through the warmth, through the wetness, and when they slip in, I write I L-O-V-E Y-O-U on the inner wall inside her, letter by letter. By the time I reach the second O, she's trembling.
>
> She writes to : I l-o-v-e y-o-u t-o-o on the terry cotton fabric of my trousers, Rs. 125 per metre, stretched tightly over my hardness. Our passions peak, the movie begins, we get up and walk out.... My trousers are stained so I pull my shirt out, but it fall below the waist. It does not look good, the end of the shirt, all crumbled up, but it covers the evidence.[8]

The 'stain' on the shirt of the hero is not only a simple stain of physical fulfilment, but it is a stain on Indian traditional cultural fabric as well as the stain on a unique concept of spirit and intellect.

Apart from presenting terror of death and horror of sex in the midst of love and passion, Raj Kamal Jha presents the theme of alienation, separation, loneliness and bewilderment. After the death of his parents, departure of his sister and Bhabani, the brother spends his life in long speculations and broodings. He broods over his pathetic alienation :

> I was younger then, this house had already emptied its two hearts into the city, father and sister, one was dead, the other had gone.... The bedspread gone. I had not myself a new bedsheet.[9]

The hero's life in the novel is the symbol of loneliness and alienation. His sharp imagination and sensitiveness compel him to think too much. He always speculates on love, sex and death, and these three forces of human existence are instrumental in initiating his boredom. There is no substitute of love, life and death in this world. Each and every human being is bound to suffer if these three realities are not realized in adequate manner. After the mystic disappearance of his sister, death of his father, departure of Bhabani, no one is accompanying him in his seclusion. His breakage with his beloved adds further melancholic dimensions in his life. She is no more a man of hopes and aspirations, and he spends his life without any vision :

> Like lonely lovers often do, I kept thinking things, I conjured up worlds where we were husband and wife, we had taken a house, all for ourselves, with a tiny garden infront. And for quite a while, everyday, I kept drawing and rewarding the same scene, filling it out with colours and noises.[10]

A man cannot hide the truth in his heart for a longer period. Dissatisfaction in life and unsatisfaction in love compel him to unfold some of the truths which are harmful of his existence. In the chapter entitled "Eight Words" the brother's heart surrenders before reality and his conscience does not allow him to twist the fact any more. The climax of his intellectual suffering is complete. His last eight words — '*I am the father of my sister's daughter*' reveal his mysticism before the public. After these eight words, the brother does need to twist the fact because he has already unburdened his soul. At this moment, Raj Kamal Jha writes :

> ....It is done, the eight words have been spoken, they have flown, each word across the city, like eight pigeons in flights, in the night, white against black, he does not have to lie any more, twist facts to flesh out his fiction, he coughs once to clear his throat, coughs twice,...he walks down the steps that lead off the stage, they are all standing now, some clapping but he does not hear because he has to be home in time for his daughter to wake up, to open her eyes.[11]

As far as the narrative technique of the novel is concerned, Raj Kamal Jha's *The Blue Bedspread* is instrumental in initiating an entirely new method of description. He narrates the past and the present experiences in interaction manner. He chapterizes his experiences in many heads entitled 'father', 'mother', 'sister', 'brother', and 'visitors'. Each chapter has uniqueness and interlinked with one-another. The mystery lies in his narrative skill and hence it is his great literary triumph.

NOTES AND REFERENCES

1. Raj Kamal Jha, *The Blue Bedspread* (Picador, 1999), p. 1.
2. *Ibid.*, p. 38.
3. *Ibid.*, p. 45.
4. *Ibid.*, p. 76.
5. *Ibid.*, p. 149.
6. *Ibid.*, p. 154.
7. *Ibid.*, p. 188.
8. *Ibid.*, p. 189.
9. *Ibid.*, p. 195.
10. *Ibid.*, p. 197.
11. *Ibid.*, pp. 227-28.

16

Novel As a Mirror of Indian Culture : A Study in Raja Rao's Fiction

PRAMOD KUMAR SINGH AND A.S. RAO

Raja Rao, born in Mysore in 1909 in an Oxthodox Brahmin family, is one of the important writers of Indian-English literature. His novels and collection of short stories contain vivid pictures of Indian rural house-holds, Hindu's folk and customs, and mythology of Hindu puranas. Along with Mulk Raj Anand and R.K. Narayan, he forms the remarkable trilogy of elder Indian English Novelists. He is poetic and metaphysical sensitive to the day to day common problems of Hindu rural folk. He is, however, not at all politically committed like Anand nor is he like R.K. Narayan.[1] The noted critic M.K. Naik rightly says that Raja is a metaphysical man whereas Mulk Raj Anand is the novelist of social man and R.K. Narayan is the novelist of individual man. Although the characters of their writings are vehicle of expression of their creative urge, the heroes of R.K. Narayan reflects the social milieu along with existing human problems, the characters of Mulk Raj Anand highlight the litigable conditions of under-dogs, whereas the characters of Raja Rao act and react with incidents to throw light on Hindu mythology and religious folkways. Rao has studied in Mysore in childhood and later graduated from Madras University before he went Europe for further education.

He is not a prolific writer like R.S. Narayan and Mulk Raj Anand. His first collection of short stories, *The Cow of Barricades* was published in 1947. His first novel *Kanthapura* was completed in 1938. His next novel *The Serpent and the Rope* was written in 1960.

Rao has himself said, he felt lost and alienated and wandered around for many years before retracing his roots and identity, thanks to the help of his Guru, Sri Atmananda.[2] *The Cat and Shakespeare* was published in 1965 and *Comrade Kirillov* in 1976. His next novel *The Chessmaster and Moves* deals with spiritual encounters between India and America. His story *The Cow of the Barricades* highlights the religious importance cow, the mother. Gauri, the sacred cow, fights the red man with non-violence. She is represented as Kamdhenu, the cow of plenty, the mother India, mother of love and compassion. She is further presented in *The Serpent and the Rope* and the mother principle. Rao in his writing links the recurrent symbols like the cow, mother and Gauri, the sacred wife of Shiva. Rama expresses his reverence in *The Serpent and the Rope* and says, "what wonderful animals these be in our sacred land such maternal and ancient looks they have. One can understand why we worship them." (p. 25) The worship of cow is integral part of Hindu's mythology since time immemorial. Aditi, the mother of the gods is described both as the cow and the mother — 'The Supreme Light' whence all radiances proceed.[3]

His first novel *Kanthapura* (1938) is a fusion of poetry, politics, religion and social reforms.[4] The novel gives an account of national movement from freedom in a small village, Kanthapura, shown to the readers through the eyes of a grandmother. The village is like another common village of South India. In a typical Indian traditional style, the narrator begins his narration, referring to the events of ancient History of India and of present times, mentioning sometimes Gods, sometimes the people existing in real life :

> "Rise up, O God of Gods; I have come to bring you sinister news. Far down on the earth you chose as your Chief daughter Bharatha, the goddess of wisdom and well-being. You have her the sage-loved Himalayas on the north and the seven surging seas to the south, and you gave her to Ganges to meditate on, the Godavary to live by, and the pure Cauvery to drink in." " — Oh sage, — pronounced Brahma, — Shiva himself will forthwith go and incarnate on the earth and free my beloved daughter...." (p. 111)

The characters of the novel represents the common people of south Indian villages. We meet with an unforgettable character like Moorthy of corner House "going through life like a noble cow" and Ratna, the child widow whose romantic relation with the hero Moorthy is submerged in the struggle for independence, the policeman Bade Khan symbolising brute nature of British Police, Venkamma the opportunist, Bhatt the moneylender and Narasamma, the pious old mother who chooses to breath her last only her son being excommunicated. In such a social milieu, an earthly God of common Indian people, Gandhi, emerges on the thematic scene of the novel. The young boy, Moorthy, is the disciple of Mahatma Gandhi who fights for the boycott of the English goods, arranges a spinning wheel from town according to the appeal of the Congress Committee, and handing over the natives of Kanthapura says, "Million and Million yards of foreign material is brought to India, but all the foreign stuffs make us poor and corrupt. It is necessary to wear cloths made out of the spinning wheel by your own hands. And this is a sacred act." (p. 112)

Moorthy's village had four and twenty houses but all houses were not big like the house of Postmaster Suryanarayan, situated by the temple corner. Like other villages of south India, social stratification existed in the village and houses were constructed in caste-wise clusters. The narrator gives caste-wise division of the villages and explains, "Till now I've spoken only of the Brahmin quarter. Our village had a Pariah quarter too, a potters' quarter, a weavers' quarter, and a Sudra quarter. How many huts had we there? I do not know. There may have been ninety or a hundred — though a hundred may be the right number. Of course, you wouldn't expect me to go to the Pariah quarter, but I have seen from the street-corner Beadle Timmayya's hut." (p. 13)

The novel may be regarded as a tribute to the Indian tradition. The novelist skilfully introduced the mythological elements in chronological order. This is why the novel of Raja Rao is often regarded as "Gandhi Purana", and K.R.S. Iyengar calls it, "a veritable grammar of the Gandhian myth — the myth that is but a poetic translation of the reality. It will always have a central place in Gandhi literature."[5] The novel written with high artistic narrative skill and definite affinity with national tradition, earned great popularity for Raja Rao when it was published in 1963. C.D. Narasimhaiah writes about the significance of Kanthapura, "for the first time in modern times in India the novel in Raja Rao's hands has become a mature means of enlarging the frontiers of human consciousness."[6]

The Serpent and the Rope (1960) is one of the finest novels written in English after 1945. The novel has far more complex fabric than that of *Kanthapura*. It is a 'classic', not merely by national but by the most exacting international standards. The noted critics like Prabhakar Machva, C.D. Narasimhaiah and E.M. Forster called it the best novel not only in Indian-English literature, but in Indian literature in general. K.R.S. Iyengar says, "If *Kanthapura* is Raja Rao's Ramayana, then *The Serpent and the Rope* is his 'Mahabhartha'."[7] The novel is a work of complex amalgamation of the cultures and religions of the East and the West, full of religious and philosophical symbolism.

The novel is largely autobiographical and refers to the early period of 1950's and the occurrences of the places and spread over India, France and England. The central character of the novel is a young historian, Ramaswamy (Rama), who is narrator of the story. The son of a professor Rama, he can read Kannada and Sanskrit at the age of just four years, and in his youth he passed M.A. in English and French. At the age of 22, he is sent to France to study the history of Europe. Rama is handsome and intelligent. He loves poetry and frequently quotes Bodelaire, Valeri, Rilke, Thoro, Emerson and Whitman. He meet a lady teacher of ancient history, Madeleine Russelin in the campus of University and this meeting soon turns into love affairs. Rama is younger to Madeleine by five years. But neither the difference of age, nor the difference of nationality or religion dearer the young Rama entering into a wedlock with the lady. The marriage, however, brings bad luck for Rama. His first child dies in early age and the second is still unborn. Thereafter, Rama's father in India passes away. The responsibilities of four sisters and brothers and step mother fall on the shoulder of Rama. He suffers from T.B. and the infection of his lungs gradually becomes more acute. Rama and Madeleine fail to sustain the sudden befallen burden of challenges in life of them. Their just few years old union breaks. Madeleine on separation becomes engaged in religious works. Rama return to his native country. Thus, the novel passes through a number of complex problems through the difficulties of Rama.

The theme of East and West encounter is obvious in the novel. The problem of marriage between a Hindu and a Christian is dealt delicately handled by the novelist. Both young hearts, born and brought up in two different religion, perceive differently most of the things in their life. Nevertheless, they are ready for a mutual compromise, endeavouring to understand the spiritual world of each other. Hence Madeleine shows her willingness to understand the Hindu religion and meaning of Brahman. She narrates to Rama an incident which took place during fascist occupation. A German officer tried to strike on her head. The moment the officer raised his hands towards her face, Madeleine smiles, and he could not do anything. She claims, "It was the Brahman in me." (p. 15) Madeleine's interest in Hindu religion aroused reciprocal feelings in Rama. He begins to study the teachings of Christianity to learn its principles. It helped him understanding the works of Dostoevsky in better way. According to Raja Rao, the spiritual union of people of two different world of religion is illusory and short lived.

REFERENCES

1. S. Krishnaswamy, *Glimpses of Women in India*, Ashish Publishing House, New Delhi, 1983, p. 30.
2. K.R.S. Iyengar, *Indian Writing in English* (Asia Publishing House, Bombay, 1972), p. 408.
3. C. Verghese Paul, *Problems of the Indian Creative Writer in English* (Somaiya, Bombay, 1971), p. 144.
4. *Ibid.*
5. K.R.S. Iyengar, *Indian Writing in English.*
6. C.D. Narasimhaiah, "Raja Rao's Kanthapura : an analysis," *The Literary Criterion* (Summer, 1966), N. 2, V. III, p. 70.
7. *Ibid.*, p. 312.

17

Feverish Fallacy : A Study of Amitav Ghosh's *The Calcutta Chromosome*

R.K. GUPTA

Amitav Ghosh's *The Calcutta Chromosome* holds its recognition as Chief d'aeuvre in the field of literature. Mr. Ghosh deals with the issue of the malarial fever in that the reputed scientist Sir Ronald Ross has got the Nobel Prize for his works on malarial fever. The term 'feverish fallacy' is applied to refer the mystical aspect of the novel. In this regard the novelist presents a principle of science and counter-science through what Murugan says :

> "You know all about matter and anti-matter, right? And rooms and anti-rooms and Christ and anti-Christ and so on?... Now let's say there was something like science and counter-science? Thinking of it in the abstract, wouldn't you say that the first principle of a functioning counter-science would have to be secrecy? The way I see it, wouldn't just have to be secretive about what it did (it couldn't hope to beat the scientists at the game any way); it would have to be secretive in what it did. It would also have to use secrecy as a technique of procedure. It would in principle have to refuse all direct communication, straight off the bat, because to communicate, to put ideas into language would be to establish a claim to know — which is the first thing that a counter-science would dispute." (88)

The novelist tries to analyse the very term feverish fallacy and secrecy thereof, and contradictions of knowledge. Further he says :

> "May be this other team started with the ideas that knowledge is self-contradictory, may be they believed that to know something, is to change it, therefore in knowing something, you've already changed what you think you know so you don't really know it at all : You only know its history. May be they thought that knowledge couldn't begin without acknowledging the impossibility of knowledge." (88)

The novelist colours the very term with obscurity and spirituality remaining almost unexplained and unrelated. He further explains that "If it's true that to know something is to change it, then it follows that one way of changing something of effecting a mutation, let's say — is to attempt to know it or aspect of it." (88) The novelist lays stress on mysticism and self-contradiction and compares it with artless awareness and method of the uneducated Indians. What is intended here is to examine how this principle of counter-science is delineated adroitly in the form of feverish fallacy.

The novelist proceeds with Murugan who is an Indian Scientist working in New York's Life — Watch, an expert on Ronald Ross and malarial fever. Murugan analyses the anecdote to Antar the Egyptian technologist working alone from his flat in New York with his computer AVA according to the directions of his employer, the International Water Council. The very story with Murugan has presented on the screen and shown to Antar who has solely to press some buttons and AVA starts hunting all the comte rends about Murugan, his ideas, his beliefs, his movements, his assumptions and logics. Antar watches it as film, as we do, on telly screen. The novel began in early 21st century in Antar's flat in New York with the presence of an ID card on AVA's screen which moved her system and she wouldn't stop till she traced out all about the theme : as Why? When? How? Where? She presents some kinds of excited urge for self-improvement. The novelist delineates this technique of avenir minutely : "Anything she didn't recognize she'd take apart on-screen, producing microscopic structural analysis, spinning the images around and around, tumbling them over, resting them on their side, producing ever greater refinements of details." (3-4) The novelist further makes it clear as, "she had been programmed to hunt out real-time information, and that was what she was determined to get. Once she'd wrung the last, meaningless detail out of him, she'd give the object on her screen, final spin, with a bizarrely human smugness, before propelling it into the horizonless limbo of her memory." (4)

The novelist has presented this mode of computer system of the future, like H.G. Wells' Time-Machine, to pass in time-past, recent past and the present for Antar. The novel presents it through the incidents that occurred in 1995 in Calcutta as also some hundred years before in Hyderabad and Calcutta. To us it is past — the last decade of the 19th century, the present days of August 1995 and the future time in earlier days of the 21st century. He has managed the space of time accordingly. In this regard Malcolm Bradbury observes time and says : "...an exploitation of relation between antecedent and present, between the time-span, of what is told and the time it takes to tell, between narrated time and narrational time, between matter attended to scenically and in detail."[1] It is time which covers only a few hours for Antar to observe Murugan's experiences of two days in Calcutta and what he shows the experiments of Ronald Ross and others, some years of the 19th century. The story proceeds through AVA and presents to the reader the three standards of time. Mr. Ghosh has tried to illustrate the oriental sense of mystery and divine belief in birth and rebirth, excellence and change of order which is nothing but a dramatic satiation — calling it a high degree of fictional technique. The novelist calls this technique the Calcutta chromosome.

The novelist presents the historical facts of Ronald Ross's experiments about malarial fever. He shows the divine power of Mangala, an assistant to D.D. Cunningham who is portrayed as a goodess-like-figure only because he has command to cure syphilis. He has also got knowledge of transcending life beyond life. In this concern two paradigms are analysed and Mangala once in 1893 performs a ritual *viz.*, "the woman Mangala was seated at the far end of the room, on a low divan, but alone and in an attitude of command, as though enthroned. By her side at the far end of the room were several bamboo cages, each containing a pigeon...they were all slumped on the floors of their cages, shivering, evidently near death...on the floor by the divan, clustered around the woman's feet, were some half-dozen people in various attitudes of supplication, some touching her feet, others lying prostrate. Two or three others were huddled against the wall, wrapped in blankets..."they were syphilitics, in final stages of the terrible disease." (125-26) Farley, a Western scientist, saw Mangala in this state and tried to understand her intrinsically. He wished to warn the people not to waste their expectations on whatever Mangala offered and opened the counterfeits to fake the common and gentle people. This makes Farley curious and so he remains there to observe the Mangala's performance of rituals. After all, in regard to his own experiments, Farley puts a question to see the transformations that Laveran presented : "It was then that hesaw Laveran's rods appear, hundreds of them, tiny cylindrical things, with their pointed penetrating heads piercing the blood maisma." (128)

Another incident takes its place when he is promised by a young boy on behalf of Mangala to reach the birth place but did not reach there : "If I would but accompany him to his birth place, fortunately the place of which he spoke is not far from the location of my clinic." (129) Even the letter he wrote had no trace of it. It forms the anecdote of Farley's and Mangala's struggle which has no scientific existence. Adroitly the novelist constructs feverish fallacy calling it counter-science. The next event occurred in 1995. The rituals which are recorded are performed on the body of Romen Haldar. Romen Haldar was to meet Sonali but he did not meet her. The reason by which he is dead is not disclosed by the novelist. Such mystery was described in the name of Calcutta chromosome : It only presents the feverish fallacy in the novel :

> "She caught a glimpse of tops of dozens of heads, some male, some female, young and old, packed in close together. Their faces were obscured by the smokes and flickering firelight.... A figure had come out of the shadows : it was a woman and she was dressed very plainly — in a crispy-starched saree, with a white scarf tied around her hair...she had a cloth bag slung over one shoulder, an ordinary cotton jhola, in her left hand she was carrying a bamboo bird-cage. She seated herself, by the fire and placed

> the bag and the bird-cage besides her. She took out two scalpels and a pair of glass plates. Then she reached out, placed her hands on whatever it was lying before the fire and smiled...there was a flash of bright metal and necklace of blood flew up and fell sizzling on the fire. (139-40)

The novelist presents another happening and mentions the murder of station-master by a boy named Laakhan in a moonless night at Renupur probably in the year 1900. Phulboni has saved herself from the train accident at Renupur in 1933 and in the same year Grigson has also saved himself from the same incident which Phulboni has faced with. Both the characters are followed by the railway station lantern and do not see who is trying to kill both of them. We see another implication of a boy Laakhan who arrives at Urmila's door wrapping fish in a paper. These experiments present nothing but the novelist describes one common principle of feverish fallacy.

The novelist presents mystical aspect of the plot which becomes wonderful to every one. If one puts the questions of why and in what direction the happenings move on, one feels perplexed caliing it bavardage. The novelist has narrated these mysterious incidents skilfully and has concluded it as feverish fallacy. At the end of the novel it is shown through the AVA that Murugan, Urmila and Sonali have moved swiftly to the station Sealdah where they are made known about Phulboni and Mrs. Arnouin who have reached before. But it is the place from where Murugan is presented as missing. The novel explains the failure of the body and migration therefrom. The novelist deals with the experiments of the ultimate transcendence of nature, of immorality : "What I'm really talking about is a technology for interpersonal transference." (90) The novelist has taken this 'feverish fallacy' as topical issue of the recurrence of the malarial fever which is highly fictitious remaining almost unexplained and unrelated. The novel presents the story of the secondary world and it does not create the experience and impression of the primary world. Jaya Banerji observes the thread of malarial experiments and says : "If Ghosh ever drew his story-line on a blackboard he would end up with real granny's knot of a plot — each character's life intertwined with the others in some way or the other. As for direction, he proceeds in ever decreasing circles until he comes to the centre which is where he started in the first place."[2] The application of the term appears far from satiation to the reader. The incidents which are mentioned in the novel has the clues that are left to the imagination and solution of the reader.

Thus, we see that against all the incidents, experiments and technical terms of the new technology, the novel presents the feverish fallacy which does not form any impression on the readers' minds as it occurs with thrillers. Even Metaphysical concept does not enhance in anyway the deeply discerned moral or aesthetic assumptions.

NOTES AND REFERENCES

1. Bradbury, Malcolm, *Possibilities : Essays on the State of the Novel,* Oxford University Press, London, 1973.
2. Banerji, Jaya, "*Review of the Calcutta Chromosome*" in *Indian Review of Books,* Vol. 5, No. 9, June-July, 1996, Madras.

18

Shobha De's *Sultry Days* : A Tale of Strange Obsessions

P.K. SINGH

Shobha De, born in Maharashtra in 1948, is one of the best novelists of recent days. She has earned world-wide reputation for her novels : *Socialite Evenings* (1988), *Starry Nights* (1990), *Sisters* (1992) and *Strange Obsession* (1992). Her non-fiction : *Surviving Man* (1997) and *Speed Post* (1999) are also known as fine fictional arts. She had the privelege of editing three leading magazines : 'Stardust,' 'Society' and 'Celebrity'.

Her *Sultry Days* (1994) is a unique love story of Nisha, an impressionable teenager college girl, and God (Deb), ragged and bearded young man, who was son of a devoted communist. She meets him in the college canteen and falls in love with him. God's uncertain and driving ambition leads him into the unreal world of pseudo-poetry, art for hire and compromised journalism. He appeased his sensual urge with her beloved Nisha and visited brothels for satisfaction of sexual urges. The father of God, called comrade, lead the processionists and courted arrest at Flora Fountain (Kala Ghada).

Nisha gets a job in an advertising company. She missed adequate love from her father and mother. But she at least felt to get a bit more love from her father than her mother. Her father too, like her, was a passionate man who love his wife but didn't get reciprocation. Nisha explains her experience of electra complex and her mother's heartlessness towards her :

> "I'm sure my father loved my mother, at least, in those days. About her I can't say. That was one

> taboo area. In any case, my mother wasn't particularly demonstrative. Neither was my father, but he did't actually shrink from physical, contact the way mother did. She stopped holding me when I was five years old, you are a big girl now, 'She'd said,' stop behaving like a baby.
>
> Papa continued to plant a vague kissor muss up my hair absently till I was much older. I missed having brother and sister. I asked my mother once why she'd stopped with me. The question had made her most uncomfortable." (p. 20)

The love and obsession of to her lover 'God' was quite strange and unusual. Usually when a gal is seen in love with someone, she cannot tolerate any third one coming between her lover and her. But Nisha is seen quite unpertubed when she comes to know about a prostitute (Bijli) slipping between them. Not even an iota of jealously is seen coming into her heart when God explains his infatuation with 'Bijli'. God asks her that he loves her too much and she, for him, is everything : mother, sister, lover, daughter etc. Shobha explains the situation :

> "When God got his bike (with money borrowed,
> scrounged or stolen, I never found out), our
> lives changed. It made him feel powerful.
> And confident.
> 'Her name is Bijli,' he told me.
> At first, I thought he was only joking.
> But no. Bijli was a person to God.
> She had feelings. She was the one
> 'woman' who understood him. Years later,
> he explained Bijli's role in his life to
> me.
> 'She was everything, yaar, Mother, sister,
> lover, daughter. I could count on her.
> I knew that if I looked after her, she'd
> look after me. And she was faithful.
> No other man ever rode my while
> she was mine." (p. 28)

When Nisha warns him that he may be defamed for living in association with an infamous and immoral prostitute, God says candidly brushing aside her suggestion, "Who cares, *yaar*? I love Bijli and she loves me — *bas*, matter ends. Why should I bother about what all these chamchas on the road must be thinking. Anyway — how does it affect their lives? or yours? Do you feel jealous?" (p. 29). He, thus shamelessly, disown the moral sanction of society and the world.

Sex and sensation is one of the favourite themes of Shobha De. While depicting sex, usual or abnormal, she never hesitates to go upto an extreme. She can talk about anything : homosexuals, prostitutes, extramarital relations, adultery, gandus (homosexual) etc. in the chapter four, she shows us as to how the "chitra Gallery was run by a homosexual couple" (p. 43) and the "man's hunger for beautiful girls matched his thirst for tea" (p. 42), Shobha narrates about the abnormal behaviour of Basu with Nisha.

Nisha explains :

> "Perhaps encouraged by my tolerance, he finally reached for my other hand under the small table and placed it squarely on his erect penis saying, "Feel my member, it is thursting for you : I hastily withdraw my hand and looked up to see whether any of the waiters had seen anything." (p. 46)

Babli, a girl of tenth standard, is seen having great curiosity seeing the prostitution area of Kamathipura. She escapes and gets married illegally with a married man, who was nearly twenty years older to her. She goes to see the brothels despite strong objection of the car driver Mrinal Laxman, and stops the car in the middle of prostitution area :

> "Laxman growled, if anything happens to the car or to any of the babylog, I'm not responsible. Remember that. I'll tell the seth that baby forced me.
>
> We absolved him of all responsibility in the matter and continued to gaze with unblinking fascination at the half-clad women hanging out of the unbelievably small cages. Which were their

> workplaces. They wore such strange costumes-thigh-length skirts with sari cholis or just brassier on top. 'They stuff their bras,' Bably told us knowledgeably. 'Most of them don't have any boobs.'
> 'Some of the girls couldn't have been much older than us. They were tiny, fragile and fair with lustrous, long hair.' 'Nepali prostitutes,' said Babli, 'they cost more because they are fair.' " (p. 50)

Nisha lived in company of God passionately and happily for above a year. Many people knew them separately and as a couple. They even bedded together without hesitation and did not care for social norms. Yet, God never expressed his genuine feelings to Nisha. God always endeavoured to show himself negatively, although he was not so in reality. He often spoke insensitive remarks about his parents, brother and even mother arousing ire of Nisha. She was amazed at the way God went out of his way to project himself so negatively. Nisha explained her relation with God and said, "though we were spending a great deal of time together, I was getting more involved in my career than I'd bargained for when I took the job. Our dirty weekends' provided a safety-valve. It was also the only time I got to be with God without hangers on milling around. This was important for me, especially our intimacies — physicals ones I mean. He was the first man I'd known, had carnal knowledge of, as they say. And God, for all his crude public conduct, was a tender lover who took care not to hurt me." (p. 75)

Anil Bhandan, a marketing guy, is another interesting character of the novel impressing Nisha. He was at his early thirties and has come back from America after working with marketing agencies in America. He spoke with a faint accent and wore sexy spectacles. He, contrary to God, was clean and motivated. He generally wore reverse-pleated trouser with tum-ups and looked very smart and chick. Anil's marketing research agency had a loose arrangement with Arti's agency and so he was at her officer at least three times a week, all slick and sexy in his Italian fit shirts and baggy trousers. Anil's office was also neat, modern and well organised. The cabins and cubicles of his office were in American system. The furniture were modular, with swivel chairs and efficient filing system. The walls were in primary colours. Nisha was curious about her bathroom because bathroom, to her, reveal so much about their users. Anil's bathroom was also found to be spotlessly clean with a cheerful shower curtain that had a rainbow on it. He was equally candid about his passion for cooking. He was able to cook many things : omlettes of various kinds, mushrooms sauteed in butter, stewed prunes, creamy champagne etc. Nisha enjoyed the joyful company of Anil during the two-week estrangement from God and it ended a morning when Bijli and he came to collect her from her home.

God is apparently, unlike Nisha, seen envious about her company with Anil. He is critical of his habits and qualities too. When Nisha asked God to marry her, he brushed aside her request and jealously suggested to get married with Anil in satirical tone. She tried her best convince him but all in vain :

> "God, please. P-L-E-A-S-E. I know you asked me to marry you. Why do you feel so ashamed now? Everybody gets married. Even communists and poets. 'Shut up, you silly woman. Who said anything about marriage? I was lagaoing line, that's all, don't take it seriously.' 'Isn't it a bit late in the day for that?'
>
> Marriage! Huh! you should marry that pansy with the fairy hair. He's more your type. You can discuss advertising and marketing in bed and get your organs reading feasibility reports. I doubt that you'll get them any other way.
>
> 'So you did get jealous.' 'Jealous of that half-cook. Don't be ridiculous. Tell me — how did you spend your evening at his place? Not that I'm interested. No — let me tell you. He talked about America and you drooled over his pizzas.' (p. 86)

Shobha highlights the increasing happenings of love-marriages between unequals in metropolitan cities. Such guys and gals marry each other in a fit of fun, they call it love, and not for money and status providing physical comforts and social recognitions. Roy is seen upset in his office because his "daughter, Janine, had run off with a sacked driver and shacked up with him at Bombay's notorious Antop Hill" (p. 88). Arti and some others in the office don't see anything wrong in it as, to them, "it's nothing more than a class war" and a "terrible nexus between the haves and have-nots. So what if he's a driver? He is also a human being" (p. 86). Roy Calls Nisha in her office's cabin and seeks her help in bringing back his cloped daughter. He wants help of God (Deb) also. He beseechs, 'I need you boyfriend's help to get my darling back. My wife is completely wrecked by this horrible affair. We trusted the rascal — and this is what he did to us — to our honour and prestige. A driver! It's disgraceful I hope our clients don't get affected by the news — it is being circulated, isn't it? — there's money to be made here. I'm willing to pay — anything — within reasonable limits, of course, to get my daughter back." (p. 90)

Shobha de does not hesitate to use unpleasant sex related words such as 'masturbation', 'fuck,' 'semen' etc. in the course of presentation of a scene or a dialogue. God behaving like a swine in chapter eight of the novel, did not hesitate to masterbate before Chandani. One day he asks Chandani as to whether she knows about semen, gets some soaps and starts masterbation in front of her. She says, 'he masterbated — right there in front of me. It was the most beautiful thing. That is called love" (p. 93). The photographer Pebbles Prabhu is seen to rough up with his models during photo-sessions if they begged for more photos. His photo-sessions were so notorious that most first-times took mommies and boyfriends alongwith them for protection. This angered Pebbles who said, "If you need bodyguard with me, you can go fuck yourself. I don't have the time to waste on you. (p. 95)

Deb (God) had some connection with powerful politicians also. He was associated with Yashwantbhai Dawani who was an influential political broker, known for his ruthless wheeling and dealing. Due to his strong political influences, he was simply called as the collector among right circles. He controlled the purse-strongs of his party and arm-twisted huge donations out of industrialists and businessmen. Everybody knew about his *modus operandi* but nobody could dared take on him. Yashwantbhai courted and pampered the press since he was aware that right mentions in the right papers would consolidate his image within the party. God has come into his contact with him at one of Iqbal's art openings. Due to Deb's such political connections, the boss of Nisha, Mr. Roy, wants his help in bringing her eloped daughter back to his home and requests Nisha for this.

Deb is later seen engaged in the film affairs. He enjoys every moment of his newly-acquired status in the film industry. When Nisha asked amusingly as to whether anybody see their films? Deb looked angrily and said, "Not the sort of people you know! But certainly — a film like Ghosh's latest — that one about a woman married to holy stone — is seen by a wide audience of discerning film-goers. He's entering it for the Berlin Film Festival. If I hadn't picked him up and promoted him — forget it, yaar. He would have still been hanging around Mandi House trying to get some good enough? Deb replied promptly, "Good? It's brilliant! What a camera work. What concept. What acting. He's one of use — he was not sold his soul to the system." (p. 121).

The novel throws light on the sexual abuse of hotel boys as well as explanation of women at different levels. Deb talks about a film in which "a woman is married to a holy stone" (p. 121). He also talks about a documentary film highlighting exploitation of boys in hotels. Nisha says to Deb :

> "Are you talking about the one who made the famous film on the exploited hotel boys in Udipi restaurants? Hahn! That female, very sexy, yaar. What a woman! Are! That film gets raves internationally. When she went to cannes, all the foreign presswallahs were sniffing around her. She's too much." (pp. 121-122)

Shobha De throws light on the hollow life and living of film and modelling world. The handling of weired clients, models and photographers were all a heartless formalities. The people of the world were mostly shameless and caved for the social sanctities. Mr. Suresh Gupta was a film producer and the most sought-after man in film world. All the stars wanted to work with him but he was a "real bastard, filthy, illiterate, thorough fellow" (p. 142). Yet everybody wanted to come and lick his dirty feet. Mr. Gupta came near Malini, a model, who glared at him and said politely, 'Fuck off'. All persons close enough to hear her words were stunned into silent. Mr. Gupta took a little drink and started abusing everybody presence — even the stars of his films. Nobody could dare to object her. They rather laughed when he started cracking coarse jokes and encourage him to drink some more. Thereafter, he rode over a deck-chair and yelled for Sonia, the beautiful young actress he was promoting. Sonia was nothing more than his slave. It was a foregone conclusion of all that Gupta had been taking undue and the fringe benefits of such an alliance. After some time, when his intoxication soared, he yelled at Sonia, "Take your sari off — what are you hiding? What are you shamed of? Haven't! seen your naked body? And hasn't the public? Come on, We all know what you look like without your cloths" (p. 143). Initially, Sonia tried to laugh it off and divert his attention. But he just stood and pulled a small pistol from his jacket and asked, "I don't like my orders to be disobeyed. If you don't remove your sari at once, I will shoot you...?" (p. 144). And without a minute's hesitation, Sonia undressed herself right there in front of hundreds of guests. She didn't even look scared. Her eyes were cold and expressionless. She just stood there, shivering a little, staring straight at Gupta. Nobody dared to move or say anything. Finally, Gupta laughed and put the gun away.

The relationship of Nisha with God (Deb) gradually becomes cold enough. God had begun to treat her like a sexless person. One day, she goes to meet Iqbal, who overpowers her for sex in the anarchic studio. He drew her close to him and his rough hands were soon tearing at her blouse while his knees were still locked between her legs. Nisha explains, thereafter, and says, "Iqbal was now down on his knees, dragging my panties down roughly. I knew it was time to scream, shout, yell, run, But I couldn't do it. I was far too scared of this madman whose eyes had dilated. Whose nostrils were flared — His hands were at my breasts, pinching, squeezing, hurting" (p. 158). She told it all to God but he hardly reacted, because sharing bed with some and other hardly matters in a metropolitan city like, Bombay.

Shobha De ironically highlights the child abuse in our country. She explains in the chapter twelve as to how a little child of a metropolitan city went to a grimmy nursery in the morning and after coming back remained locked up till their mother came back late in the evening, exhausted, irritable and in no condition to deal with emotional problems. She also shows us as to how little boys are sold to Sheikhs for camel racing or buggering" (p. 183). In the chapter fifteen, God was seen shot at by mafia dons. The fatal bullet had entered his stomach and lodged itself in his spinal cord. It took nearly ten days for him to recover enough to get out of ICU and to the general ward. But he finally passed away leaving the heartless people of the world. The novel, thus, is a fine picturisation of life and culture of metropolitan cities, like Bombay.

REFERENCES

1. Shobha De, *Sultry Days* (Penguin Books, New Delhi, 1994).
2. Shobha De, *An Interview with Hindustan Times*, Nov. 21, 1999.

19

Kamala Markandaya's *Possession* : A Revaluation

SHAYAM S. AGARWALLA

Kamala Markandaya is one of three most outstanding South Asian Novelist, living in the West. Born in Mysore, graduated from the University of Madras, she has settled in the United Kingdom in 1948. Married to Mr. Taylor (an Englishman), she has a daughter. A roaming father helped her to observe a cross-section of people in Europe. Like Santha Rama Rau and Bharati Mukherjee she is intensely aware — even self-conscious — regarding her position as a writer, writing the lives of immigrants and expatriates. She had lived her bachelor life in colonial India, and married life in England. Therefore, her handlong of the East-West encounter is as realistic as that of Chaman Nahal, Nayantara Sahgal, Manohar Malgonkar and T.N. Murari.

Literature is an important "Contact Zone", to use Mary Louise Pratt's term, where "transculturation" takes place in all its complexity. Plays such as Shakespeare's *Othello* and *The Tempest* evoke contemporary ideas about the bestiality or incivility of non-Europeans. Or, *The Tempest* depicts the dehumanisation of colonial rule. Gauri Vishwanathan's book, *Masks of Conquest*, tells us that English literary studies became a mask for economic and material exploitation, and were an effective form of political control. One form of this argument had been put forward by imperial historians who claimed that English literature (especially Shakespeare) and English education in general, had fostered ideas of liberty and freedom in native populations. It took Western Enlightenment notions of democracy and fraternity to make Indians or Africans demand equality for Themselves! This dynamic is perhaps best symbolized by Shakespeare's Caliban, who tells Prospero and Miranda :

> You gave me language, and my profit on't.
> Is, I know how to curse. The red-plaguerid you
> for learning me your language!
>
> (i, ii, 363-65)

Caliban can curse because he has been given language by his captors. The illustration of Caliban is as much valid for Latin America as it is for India and Africa. Kamala Markandaya, like Ariel, is "a creature of the air, although also a child of the isle, is the intellectual."[1] Both Caliban and Ariel are the intellectuals in neo-colonialism. So is Kamala Markandaya.

Markandaya's possession (1963), according to K.R.S. Iyengar, is "something of a parable of colonialism, the passing of an empire, and the current insidious movement of 'neo-colonialsm'."[2] The word colonialism, according to Oxford English Dictionary, comes from the Roman 'colonia' which meant 'farm' or 'settlement', and referred to Romans who settled in other lands but still retained their citizenship. Accordingly, the OED describes it as,

> a settlement in a new country...a body of people who settle in a new locality, forming a community subject to or connected with their parent state, the community so formed, consisting of the original settlers and their descendants and successors, as long as the connection with the parent state is kept up.

The process of 'forming a community' in the new land necessarily meant unforming or reforming the communities that existed there already, and involved a wide range of practices including trade, plunder, negotiation, warfare, genocide, enslavement and rebellions. "So colonialism can be defined as the conquest and control of other people's lands and goods... Modern colonialism did more than extract tribute, goods and wealth from the countries that it — conquered it restructured the economies of the latter, drawing them into a complex relationship with their own, so that there was a flow of human and natural resources between colonised and colonial countries.... In whenever direction human beings and materials travelled, the profit always flowed back into the so-called 'mother country'."[3]

Gareth Griffiths earmarks the role of colonizers by explaining the role played by Orientalism written by Edward Said :

> Said's concern is the relationship between textual representations and social practice... Said argued that colonialism created non-mutual and hierarchis relations in which the colonizer was always and inescapably the Self to the marginalized other of the colonized.... In other words the colonized could be literally moulded into whatever best served the economic and political purposes of the colonizer."[4]

Kwame Nkrumah, the first President of independent Ghana, coined term "neo-colonialism". "The essence of neo-colonialism", wrote Nkruman, "is that the State which is subject to it is, in theory, independent and has all the outward tappings of International sovereignty. In reality its economic system and thus its political policy is directed from the outside."[5]

When I examine Markandaya's *Possession*, in the light of above-mentioned observations of critics, I find that Caroline is not a colonizer. First of all, she does not show any disdain for Valmiki's art. Secondly, Fanon writes that colonised people are not simply those whose labour has been appropriated but those "in whose soul an inferiority complex has been created by the death and burial to its local cultural originality,"[6] Caronline does not create any inferiority complex in Valmiki. On the contrary, she projects the art of Valmiki on to the fashionable and glittering Western world. Valmiki is simply a passive peasant boy, crude and unshaped, his goathered life well seen in his shyness "rags, goat-smell and all." His society rejects him. He appears to be an idiot to his community for he does not perform the daily chores that his class of people do and chooses to "idle" away his time in coasteful activities, such as painting and drawing on rocks and caves. Caroline, sensing talent in him, takes him ways from his parents, "compensates" them for the loss of a labour, takes him to London, Switzerland, France, Italy and Greece. Valmiki is incisive, articulate, impulsive, and artful. Kamala Markandaya's authorial *alter ego*, Anasuya, comments :

> In a way I couldn't help admiring him — this nobody in rags who was not to be moved by Caroline, whose birthright had been to get her own way, matching her inherited arrogance with an arrogance of his own which came from God knows where.[7]

The moral degradation of Valmiki starts when he enters into a passionate exploitation of Ellie, seeking her love first and then giving her a child with no sense of responsibility. His second mistress, Annabel, deserts him :

> "You ran away," she said again with a kind of cold vengeance. "You got her into trouble and you got out quick before the whiff of suicide could offend your nostrils and curt up those holy eastern sentiments of yours about the sanctity of life.... You wouldn't even know what decency means."[8]

His loss of decency, his immorality, his lust for money and fame, degenerates him internally, "Nothing, he repeated, that is the truth, Suya. If you could look inside me you would find nothing but deadwood."[9] Caroline is not responsible for his awareness of the loss of his local talent and originality. It is he who has embroiled himself with Ellio and Annabel. Thus he, enervated, entrapped, enfeebled, impoverished, imprecates evil upon himself and returns to India.

Markandaya's *Possession* is not an insidious story of neo-colonialism. Vamiki's journey from a remote and small village of South India to London, Switzerland, France, Italy and Greece under the guardianship of Caroline is not an instance of neo-colonialism, if one is to go by the definition of neo-colonialism by Nkrumah. Valmiki is Caliban and Caroline is Prospero. She taught him language and he can now curse her. She gave him name, fame, money and status. If he had remained in that remote and small village he would have died unsung, unwept, unknown like villagers in Thomas Gray's "Elegy written in a country Churchyard". Caliban would have remained savage, crude, illiterate. Prospero has done a singular service to Caliban.

Dieter Riemenschneider says that Caroline is a neo-colonialist whose "aim remains to take advantage of and to continue alienating

Indians from their own culture.... She fails to understand the religious, and thus functional, value of Val's art but looks at his paintings merely as commodities to be bartered in the market and not as man's self-expression of his communion with the divine."[10] Riemenschneider goes on to say that Caroline is materialist and, therefore, she fails to understand the spiritual Valmiki. All Westerners are materialists and all Indians are spiritualists, is the refrain of the Western and the Indian writers. Let me quote, some important lines from Ashis Nandy :

> On the one hand the British saw the Indians as overly this-worldy-Greedingly shrewd, greedy, self-centred, money-minded. On the other hand, they also despised the Indian as overly other-worldly-not fit for the world of modern science and technology, statecraft and productive work .... India is not merely its spiritual self.... The plethora of empirical studies done from Marxist as well as structural-functional vantage grounds should have at least made us aware that underlying much Indian spirituality lie this-worldly choices, hard self-interest, and reality-testing.[11]

I do not agree with Dieter Riemenschneider nor does Nandy. Valmiki's father was given compensation by Caroline for his journey to the West. Valmiki himself was willing to migrate to the West for this "self-interest, and reality-testing". He was neither in communion with the divine nor a geriatrician as to serve his parents and the Swamy. He was, in the eyes of the villages, a wastrel in the wasteland, neither a goathered nor a money-earner. Caroline picked him up to become a first-class painter. Hundreds of Indians — poets, scholars, doctors, engineers have achieved fame and names in the West because the West has provided them intellectual climate, financial contentment, and social climbing. Caroline ought to be congratulated. On the contrary, she is condemned by critics.

D. Maya says that *Possession* is an allegory on imperialism. I do not agree with her. The OED defines "imperial" as simply "pertaining to empire", and "imperialism" as the "rule of an emperor, especially when despotic or arbitrary, the principal or spirit of empire, advocacy of what are held to be imperial interests".[12]

Lenin and Kantsky had given a new meaning to the word "imperialism". Lenin predicted that in due course the lack of capital in the colonies would fall into the bag of European financial capitalists. It is this Leninist definition that allows some people to argue that capitalism is the distinguishing feature between colonialism and imperialism. The imperial country is the "metropole" from which power flows, and the colony or neo-colony is the place which it penetrates and controls.

Caroline lives in a metropolitan city and Valmiki lives in a God-forsaken place. She comes to this God-forsaken village and discovers the talent of Valmiki. She has capital but he has not. Schumpeter's political theory of imperialism slips not merely toward moralizing, but also toward metaphysical notions of human nature (the lust for power or domination). Mark the difference between physical and metaphysical notions of human nature. The question arises : is the possession of Valmiki by Carilone physical or metaphysical? Does Caroline want the physical possession to Valmiki? No. Does she want to dominate him as Howard Clinton wants to dominate his Indian workers? No. To say that Valmiki was unconsciously and innocently possessed by Caroline is to underrate the basic instinct and subtlety of an Indian boy who can fall in love with Ellie and Annabel, who knows the difference between "bought" and "compensated". When he realizes his own inner degeneracy and says to Anasuya : "Nothing," he repeated. 'That is the truth, Suya. If you could look inside me you would find nothing but deadwood'. Valmiki's debauchery, carefree, and unprofessional act, bring about his degeneracy and his flight back to India is as much an example of escapism as an example of thousands of dissolute Indians returning to India, empty-handed and empty-headed.

The Swamy is a fake. He says to Caroline : "He (Valmiki) works for that, and therein is the glory...it gives men a satisfaction so rich they cannot explain it, and mostly they do not even wish to."[13] The Swamy wants Valmiki to wander aimlessly in the waste and to achieve spiritual union with God! Kamala Markandaya had written this novel in 1963, when India was in the romantic period of economic development led by Nehru. Writing a critique of *Possession* in the twentieth-first century, in the age of globalization, fierce competition, rush for acquisition of knowledge, fame, and money, the answer of the Swamy to Caroline is nothing short of sophism. On the other hand, the urging of Caroline to tepid Valmiki was between the sough of the Swamy and the thunder of Caroline. He unfortunately opted for the former.

The orthodox Hindus in the eighteenth and nineteenth centuries considered any visit to England as paap or sin. Every Englishman was a Mlechha. The Swamy thinks that England has sapped the creativity in Valmiki. This is patently wrong. When Green, Forster, and Eliot introduced Narayan, Anand, and Desani respectively to the Western world, they had no axes to grind. When W.B. Yeats introduced Tagore to the West, it was done with a noble purpose. Greene, and Forster were the citizens of an imperial country. Not only that, *The Heart of the Matter* and *A Passage to India* are cited as allegory on colonialism. Eliot came from a colonized country in the world which he could shine. Yeats was an Irish and Ireland was under the subjugation of England. Greene, Forster and Eliot are praised, whereas Caroline is pinfolded.

A critic has said that the liberation of Valmiki from Caroline is like the liberation of India from the British rule. A very ridiculous argument, *Possession*, unlike *Midnight's Children* is not a national allegory, in the words of Frederic Jameson.

I would conclude my critique of *Possession* by emphasising that it is neither an allegory on colonialism, neo-colonialism, and imperialism nor a national allegory on India's Freedom. Caroline does not take "Possession" of Valmiki. The Swamy is a fake, who thrives on innocents like Valmiki. I would say emphatically that the Swamy "possesses" Valmiki, physically and metaphysically. That brings about the ruination of Valmiki as a budding painter.

REFERENCES

1. Roberto Ferandez Retarnar, "Caliban : Notes towards a Discussion of Culture in Our America, "tr. Lymn Garafola *et al.*, in *Massachusetts Review* 15 (Winter-Spring). 1974, p. 28.

2. K.R.S. Iyengar, *Indian Writing in English*, New Delhi : Sterling, 1962 (Fifth Edition, 1985), p. 445.

3. Aria Loomba, *Colonialism/Postcolonialism*, London : Routledge, 1998, pp. 2-4.

4. Gareth Griffiths, "The Post-colonial Project : Critical Approaches and Problems", *New National and Post-colonial Literautres*, ed. Bruce King, Oxford : Clarendon Press, 1986, p. 165.
5. Kofi Buenor Hadjor, *The Penguine Dictionary of Third World Terms*, London : Penguin, 1992, p. 215.
6. Frantz Fanon, *Black Skin, White Masks*, Frons. C.L. Marka, New York : Grove Press, 1967, p. 18.
7. Kamala Markandaya, *Possession*, Bombay : Gaico, 1967, pp. 22-23.
8. *Ibid.*, p. 207.
9. *Ibid.*, p. 212.
10. Dieter Reimenschneider, "British Characters in Indo-English Fiction", in *Aspects of Indian Writing in English*, ed. M.K. Naik, New Delhi : Macmillan, 1979, p. 146.
11. Ashis Nandy, *The Intimate Enemy*, New Delhi : OUP, 1983 (Thirteenth Impression), 1999, pp. 80-81.
12. *Possession*, p. 212.
13. *Ibid.*, p. 232.

20

Salman Rushdie's *The Ground Beneath Her Feet* : The Theme of Love, Life & Death

K.K. SINGH

Salman Rushdie's *The Ground Beneath Her Feet* (1999) can easily be considered as his best novel for several reasons, firstly for his better handling of themes of love, sex and passion and secondly, for his better artistic use of vocabulary. In his other novels like Grimus, *Midnight's Children*, *Shame*, and *The Satanic Versus* Salman Rushdie has presented himself as a man who is critical of religious, social, political and economic ridden systems of the world. His critical approach towards these things makes him controversial, but *The Ground Beneath Her Feet* surpasses all these things and comes out as a perfect piece of art. This novel is thematically based on human concerns *i.e.* realities of human existence, love, sex, passion and death are presented in beautiful manner without any ironical touch. It is a very exciting novel, hugely ambitious and original. There is lovely presentation of Rushdie's fictional imagination and its story swings between culture, modern life and ancient myths. It is a dramatic, playful and extremely moving novel comprising lovable characters of different classes.

In this novel, Rushdie has covered a vast cultural canvas-oriental culture of the East in which the Indian culture is an authentic representative, the European civilization where England is in authoritative role and the American world where the United States of America has now in position to influence the rest. Apart from presenting the love story of Ormus Cama and Vina Apsara, Rushdie has beautifully presented some other things also — now life has become problem to itself. The journey of the novel starts in India, flowers in England, and dooms in America. In this way, we come across a large number of characters both Indians and foreigners — all of them are in search of something 'new' in their life.

The Love-Story of Ormus Cama and Vina Apsara has everything — vigour and vitality on the one hand, and suffering and Mythology on the other. He was a sensitive boy right from the beginning of his childhood, and he takes interest in songs and music emotionally. He had no time for family which includes his father Sir Darius Cama, mother Spenta Cama, and his two brothers Virus Cama and Cyrus Cama. Virus Cama lived in silence because his head was struck by a cricket ball drove by his father while playing on important match. Cyrus Cama is critical of everything, and of murderous nature. Sir Darius Cama spent much time in study of philosophy and mythology, and therefore, it was lady Spenta Cama who ran the house smoothly.

Ormus Cama came into contact with Vina Apsara when Vina Apsara was only eight years old. In the beginning, the love-affair between Ormus Cama and Vina Apsara was not welcomed by surroundings. The more they hate their love, the more they become closer to each other. Ormus Cama looses interest in his family after coming into contact with Vina Apsara :

> Such were the factors that detached Ormus Cama from the ordinary ties of family life. The ties that strange us, which we call love. Because of the loosening of these ties he became, with all the attendant pain of such becoming free. But love is what we want, not freedom. What then is the unluckier man? The beloved, who is given his heart's desire and must forever after fear its loss, or the free man, with his unlooked for liberty, naked an alone between the captive armies of the earth.[1]

Vina Apsara was nourished by Piloo Doodhwala after her mystic arrival in India in very tender age. Her life is the symbol of mystery, struggle and suffering. Umeed merchant's parents deeply loved Vina. They did not check Vina's advances towards Ormus. Vina, being more sentimental and emotional, pathetic and compassionate, falls in love with Ormus Cama, and neglects Umeed's advances.

The relationship between Ormus Cama and Vina Apsara is the symbol of passion on the one hand, and their aspiration for the west on the other. They realise that India is not the proper palace where their ambitions and dreams could be fulfilled. In the words of Vina :

> Ormus Cama and I, growing up in India, felt our hearts striving towards the West, how strange it is to think of vine's early years under the aegis of that good plain man with his lust for the East, or at least its hairy breasts.[2]

The Ground Beneath Her Feet is full of love, sex and violence. It is not only a simple love story between Ormus Cama and Vina Apsara. In this novel, Salman Rushdie treats human passions and emotions in dramatic and practical manner. His greatness as a novelist lies in his dramatic fusion of dream and reality. Ormus Cama's dream to possess Vina had become reality. Ormus Cama loved Vina in Petrarchian manner, and Vina responded in semi-Petrarchian way. At the end, apart from some paradoxes, like typical Indian lover and beloved, they made for each other. Their love made them one soul in two human bodies :

> He (Ormus Cama) loved her like an addict : the more of her he had, the more he needed. She loved him like a student, needing his good opinion, playing up to him in the hope of drawing forth the magic of his smile. He was her seriousness, he was the depths of her being.[3]

The role of music and song was extremely important in their love. These are supposed to be two natural agents, and inspire them to love each other. They wanted to be singers of name and fame, and it is their ambition which compels them to become close to each other. They succeeded in their aim, and their joint effort made them world-wide famous. Wherever they performed their programme, they became famous :

> The minute Ormus Cama and Vina Apsara opened their mouths and began to sing, everybody just

> stopped thinking about anything else. When they had finished, the audience was cheering wildly.[4]

The growing fame of Ormus Cama and Vina Apsara made Umeed Merchant jealous because he also loves Vina Apsara deeply and passionately although, she did not love him. Here, Umeed Merchant began to chase the body and spirit of Vina. His inferiority complex made him more jealous, and he was ready to do anything to possess her as he himself admitted :

> From the start my place was in a corner of their live, in the shadow of their achievements. Yet I will always believe I deserved better. And there was a time when I almost had it. Not just Vina's body, but her attention.[5]

In The Ground Beneath Her Feet, the novelist handles the themes of love and death. In this novel, his main concerns are love, life and death. These three are the realities of human existence. Nobody can even imagine to live in this world without these trinity of culture. There are a large number of agents of love, life and death, which can either promote or distort human being. Salman Rushdie believes that love and life cannot be cut short by death — the supreme reality :

> Death is more than love or is it. Art is more than love or is it. Love is more than death and art, or not. This is the subject. This the subject.[6]

The Ground Beneath Her Feet is an exciting story hovering around past and present. Its narrative dances like the fates of Ormus Cama and Vina Apsara. In this novel, Salman Rushdie has given epic treatment to love, life and death — through appropriates intermingling of myth and reality. In this regard; Hermione Lee writes in *Observer* :

> *The Ground Beneath Her Feet* is very exciting and inspiring novel, hungly ambitious and original...there is a lovely freedom and penache in the way it swings between popular culture and high artfulness, modern life and ancient myth. It is dramatic, playful and extremely moving.[7]

Salman Rushdie treats the immortality and sublimity of love and art in Keatsian manner. Love never dies although the lover and the beloved will be no more after some time. This novel deals with several deaths and murders but his presentation of love between Ormus Cama and Vina Apsara overshadows all these incidents like influence of Umeed Merchant, struggle of Spenta Cama, philosophical leanings and longings of Sir Darius Cama and his tragic demise, dancing fate of Ormus Cama's two brothers. Rushdie clearly insisted that death cannot influence love because love is beyond death's reach. Vina Apsara and Ormus Cama transcend themselves above death only account of their sublime love. It is a reason that Ormus Cama's love became more sublime and elevated and everlasting too for Vina Apsara after her tragic death. Umeed Merchant rightly says :

> Ormus Cama's thoughts turn more and more towards Vina, the Vina that exists only in his imagination, who knows more intimately than any living being, is confronted on the stage of that some imagination by another Vina, her adult self, her unknown twin. Life has happened to her and turned her into a stranger. New life, and the external haunting of the past.[8]

Umeed Merchant, known as Rai, is the victim of the relationship between Ormus Cama and Vina Apsara. Like everyone, he wanted to catch the glimpse of Vina or we can say, want to get her love and body at any cost. But on the other hand, Vina did not appreciate his lustful advances. He himself considers as a culprit who always wished to influence their sublime love. Umeed Merchant, being conscious of Vina's power, reveals her attitude :

> It is almost fourteen years since our first night of love back in old Bombay and still Vina lies unclothed on our hot bed without so much as a sheat to cover her. Another sleeping beauty waiting for her prince (not me, not me) to come.[9]

Ormus Cama's oath of celibacy for ten years and is decision not to establish sexual relationship with Vina Apsara sublimates his love towards her. The elevated and sublime nature of their love make them such a union in which there is no question of identity. They have one soul existing in two bodies. They love each other for love only and not to get anything else as Salman Rushdie writes :

> The relationship of Vina Apsara and Ormus Cama expresses the tension between wisdom and eloquence. And the intervals of the Ormic guitar may well be, mathematically speaking, the structural basis not only of the whole universe but of the human soul as well. When we explore our inner space, as both Buddhists and sub-atomic physicists agree, we find a microcosmos : Ormus's music reveals to our hearts the identity of the little and the large.[10]

The role of music is extremely important in the life of Ormus Cama and Vina Apsara. Rushdie conceives music as the symbol of continuity of life itself. It is music which unites Vina and Ormus and it is music which makes them immoral forever. Their marriage is the realization of their dreams. It is love which makes them one. They have very loftier ideas about love, and of music, which is the sound of love. In this novel, love has been presented in paradoxical manner because it is love which is responsible for their separation. But after marriage, Ormus Cama and Vina Apsara wrote about love in these words :

> Love is the relationship between levels of reality. Love produces harmony and is the ruler of the arts.
>
> Love is the attempt to impose order on chaos, meaning on absurdity.
>
> Love is invactive, double naturally holding the keys to everything. There is love in the cosmos love raises us above the limitations of our bodies and gives us free will.
>
> We assert love as a cosmic force, bringing about creation.
>
> Songs are love's enchantment. They are everyday magic. The 'Sirens' song drew men to their deaths. Calypso's song kept Odysseus enchanted by her side.

> Songs enchant away our pain. Love is harmony. Harmony is love.[11]

Whereas Ormus Cama's love towards Vina is the symbol of life and sublimity, Rai's love towards Vina is the symbol of lust and nothing else. He does not love the art and spirit of Vina, rather he loves the beauty and body of Vina. Rai's attitude towards Vina Apsara is revealed by Rai himself in these words :

> These are the breasts of the woman I love. I place my nose between them and inhale their pungency, their ripeness. I place my cock between them and feel their swollen caress.[12]

All his life, Rai, like Ormus Cama kept on loving Vina Apsara. But he did not succeed in his mission. He failed in his mission because his love towards Vina Apsara lacked sublimity. Love depending on physical lust cannot remain everlasting, it is bound to be transitory. Rai's love for Vina has no ground as it ought to be. He himself confessed :

> All my life, I worshipped her. Her golden voice, her beauty's beat. How she made me feel, how she made me real, and the ground beneath her feet. I admit also that Ormus's love for Vina Apsara was greater than mine, for while I had mourned Vina as I had never mourned any loss I had, after all begun to love again. But his (Ormus) was a love which no other love could replace.[13]

Rushdie's brilliance lies in his parellel handling of myth and reality. His comparison of Orpheus and Ormus Cama is not far from reality. Salman Rushdie's emphasis on Platonic love echoes his concern towards this sublime subject. He writes :

> The god's honour zeal and heroic excellence towards love! But Orpheus...they sent back unfulfilled from Hades, showing him a phantom of the women...who did not venture to die for the sake of love, as did Alcastis, but rather devised a means of entering Hades while still alive.[14]

Salman Rushdie compares Orpheus and Ormus again and again. Both Orpheus and Ormus Cama failed to save their counterparts from disaster. Like Orpheus, Ormus Cama's effort ended in vain in his search of his beloved Vina Apsara :

> Is the failure of Orpheus to rescue her a token of the inevitable fate of love (it dies) : or of the weakness of art (it cannot raise the dead); of platonic cowardice; or of the obduracy of the so to speak gods (they harden their hearts against lovers).[15]

Unlike Rushdie's other novels. *The Ground Beneath Her Feet* is a complete artistic achievement. It has no serious ethical, political social, and economical implications. The greatness of the novel lies in its covering of vast canvas, *i.e.,* entire world : India, Europe and America. The novel compares myth and reality, past and present by realising dreams into reality through epic treatment. Ruth Padel rightly comments on this novel in *Independent* :

> *The Ground Beneath Her Feet* is a fabulous, glowing, witty and brilliant epic. This novel is about the blurring of every frontier; dour death, East and West, imagination and reality, about fame, death defying love and the nature of spin; about celibacy, corruption and alternative realities. This is Ulysses of rock 'n' roll.[16]

The greatness of Salman Rushdie lies in his presentation of a variety of characters and their hope, aspiration, frustration and suffering. Since this novel covers very vast canvas, the characters present the complexity of thoughts, visions and dreams. Their struggle to survive themselves from modern implications is presented in epic manner and it is the quality that elevate *The Ground Beneath Her Feet* from Rushdie's other novels. Don Delillo rightly says :

> Salman Rushdie's *The Ground Beneath Her Feet* is a wonderful story-telling beast that feeds on pop culture, misfit history and the persistence of myth. His epic range has never been more impressive. Here is a great novelist operating as a master of metasimorphosis transforming life, art and language in the subterranean maze of metasimorphosis —

> transforming life, art and language in the subterranean maze of his imagination.[17]

REFERENCES

1. Salman Rushdie, *The Growth Beneath Her Feet* (Vintage, U.K. 1999), p. 57.
2. *Ibid.*, p. 113.
3. *Ibid.*, p. 123.
4. *Ibid.*, p. 151.
5. *Ibid.*, p. 175.
6. *Ibid.*, p. 221.
7. Hermione Lee, *Observer*, New Delhi.
8. Salman Rushdie, *The Ground Beneath Her Feet*, p. 325.
9. *Ibid.*, p. 395.
10. *Ibid.*, p. 431.
11. *Ibid.*, p. 465.
12. *Ibid.*, p. 506.
13. *Ibid.*, p. 523.
14. *Ibid.*, p. 549.
15. *Ibid.*, pp. 550-51.
16. Ruth Padel, *Independent,* London (U.K.).
17. Don Delillo, *Sunday Mail*, London (U.K.).

21

Exposition of the Theme of Hunger in Kamala Markandaya's *Nactar in a Sieve*

PRADIPSINH B. RATHOD

> ...In India the countryside too has been polluted but not by the encroachment of industry...the pollution comes from within, through starvation.
>
> —Kai Nicholson[1]

The writer's expression taking place through social perspectives has been an integral part of fiction in general and authors in particular like R.K. Narayan, Mulk Raj Anand, Bhabani Bhattacharya, Kamala Markandaya — a few to mention out of a galaxy of Indian writers writing in English. The mere fact, that the life represented by them revolves around the fictionalization of sociological aspects, establishes a clearcut demarcating note on the reciprocal relationship between the two worlds of the writer : the ideal and the actual one. And thus, a disequilibrium caused by the dissatisfaction of the ideal world stands in thorough opposition to the real motifs.

In this regard, Kamala Markandaya's *Nectar in a Sieve* — Often compared with Bhabani Bhattacharya's *So Many Hungers* for the theme of degradation of humanity with Pearl S. Buck's *The Good Earth* for the treatment of milieu, with Dennis Stoll's *The Dove Found No Rest* for the depiction of social chaos and with Prem Chand's *Godan* for its realistic approach — presents a spectrum of themes which reflect the plight of the ideal as well as the actual world conceived by her. No doubt, the novel chiefly deals with hunger and poverty at its best; still it remains an assemblage of the rural problems such as flood, draught, famine, superstition, illiteracy, social inequalities and injustice, exploitation, struggle for survival and so on. These various aspects need, of course, a stupendous setting to create an everlasting cinematic effect. Markandaya's creation of an all time Indian village fulfils this necessity. The unbaptized South Indian village of Mankandaya symbolizes any rural area existing on Indian soil. It stands as a symbol for the socio-economic/cultural/spiritual and to some extent, socio-psychic upheavals — the inseparable ingredients of India's country people. What is most remarkable is the full-balanced togetherness of these elements; and here lies the actual force of Markandaya's rural realism.

Nectar in a Sieve runs with the protagonist-narrator Rukmani, a peasant woman suffering almost all the time within the duration of the narrative. Her family consists of her husband — Nathan, poor tenant farmer, a daughter — Ira, and six sons. Although poverty-sticken, they are happy and mutually compromised with the conditions they are put into by fate. But the establishment of the tannery initiates miseries for them. Along with this human brain-child, attached they find capriciousness of nature accompanied by cruel dealings of their landlord. Such miseries bring their apparent peace to disaster. The unwelcome entry of industrialization not only —

> ...invaded our village with clatter and din, had taken from us the maidan where our children played, and made the bazar prices too high for us.[2]

— but also intruded the complete innate atmosphere and the village economy causing devastating social calamity.

Rukmani stands in thorough opposition even to a single thought of the tannery, as it has been tempting the simple village folk into greed and immoral acts. Her fears turn true as not merely the society, but her own family is discolated, initially with two of her sons' joining the tannery as workers notwithstanding their father's much awaited desire of farming together with them. However, this separation brings in thin layer of happiness — perhaps the best period in their lives — to the family and temporarily they get rid of perpetual fear of starvation and relish some luxuries foreign/

unaffordable to them until both the brothers are dispelled from the tannery. Both of them ultimately go to Ceylon as labourers, never to return.

Apart from the man-made misfortunes, the family suffers from the pitiless hand of nature which was never merciful on them. Flood and draught destroy crops one by one. Rukmani painfully recalls :

> It was as if nothing had ever been but rain..., Nathan and I watched with heavy hearts while waters rose and rose, and the tender green of paddy field sank under and was lost...there will be little eating done this year. (43-44)

The whim of nature shifts its form again, but the result remains the same :

> ...(drought) continued until we lost count of time. Day after day the pitiless sun blazed down scorching whatever still struggled to grow and baking the earth hard until it split and great irregular fissures gaped in the land. Plants died and grasses rotted, cattle and sheep crept to the river that was no more and perished there for lack of water... (81)

Stability never sets on them after such a series of tragic periods and there can hardly remain any demarcating line between wandering hungry animals in search of food and human beings facing starvation. Hunger observes dictums neither of humanity nor of quality :

> Thereafter we fed on whatever we could find.... Early and late my sons roamed the countryside, returning with few bamboo shoots, a stick of sugarcane left in some deserted field, or piece of coconut picked from the gutter.... It was not enough, sometimes from sheer rebellion we ate grass although it was always resulted in stomach cramps and violent retching. (91)

Even the much sustained human relationships tend to lose their significance for the worst juncture if stomachs are empty :

> ...other farmers and their families in like plight to ourselves, were also out searching for food; and for

> every edible plant or root there was a struggle — a desperate competition that made enemies of friends and put an end to humanity. (91)

Still a sigh of solace is possible and practical as well if the disaster is caused by nature only, but tenant farmers like Nathan must not be rested as they have to settle the life long unsettled accounts with their landlords. The one that Nathan has, is never late in demanding and accumulating his dues, nor he troubles his mind to take a note of his tenant farmer's misfortunes and failure of his crops. This exploitation immediately results in permanent hunger and starvation; and their onerous eviction from the tenant land proves the last nail in the Nathans' coffin. Soon the couple, Rukmani and Nathan, is compelled to leave the village and live with one of their sons, Murugan, in the city where they are eventually informed of his deserting the city as well as his family. So they live on charity for some time before doing some crummy jobs; one of which succumbs Nathan to death. Despaired, Rukmani returns to the village still with "*fear of dark future : fear of sharpness of hunger; fear of the blackness of death.*" (83)

The delineation of the theme of hunger obviously remains one of the remarkable features of *Nectar in a Sieve*, chiefly due to Markandaya's first hand dealing with what she offers. She had been an independent onlooker who witnessed the socio-economic conditions of the village life during her inhabitance in South India. This meticulous fact evidently makes the novel a vital documentation of poverty and starvation caused by inhumane exploitations. Thus the theme is dealt with more comprehensive, more sympathetic and more realistic treatment when compared to some other post-independence novels where the struggle is between man and an extremely overpowering sufferings caused by starvation. The realism of the rural India lie behind the depiction of the heroic struggles made by the Nathans against the human as well as natural oddities, which in their turn, raise the novel to the lofty heights of epical dimensions. As the hero in an epic undertakes wars against his enemies, the Nathans of Markandaya undertake an everlasting war against hunger. Their struggle happens to be more poignant since their response to the forces of destruction is a sheer act of existence.

Ironically, this struggle against starvation and poverty continues relentlessly during the Nathan-Rukmani's stay in the city. Their life there is nothing but hell because of the wickedness and horrible harsh realities of society which ultimately force them to resort to begging, live among thieves and do some petty jobs — a vigorous record of iniquitous exploitations. If the statement is stretched further, some more equally prominent themes such as deterioration and debasement of humanity and devaluation of morality erupt into side-effects of hunger. The same vicious circle entangles beautiful Kunthi in prostitution and compels her to blackmail Rukmani for a handful of rice; provokes Raja, one of Rukmani's sons, to steal from the tannery only to be killed by the authority; and despairs Ira to sell her body to the tannery people in her desperate efforts to save her youngest brother from starving.

While dealing with such central ideas behind her creative impulse, Markandaya has simultaneously been developing her own world of the proletariats with the passage of time which, according to Cowasjee and Shahane is "tempered with common sense and sound judgement,"[3] and thus, her themes come out as her actual concerns for the unhappy and poverty-stricken people exploited by the bourgeoisie as well as by the misfortunes caused by nature. Markandaya's range of observations does not merely signify the truth which she witnesses — the commoners' fruitless attempts to rise above the hunger and their struggle against socio-economic upheavals — but enriches her art of story telling as well and that also to such an extent that the novel stands as her moral platform. In its turn, this standpoint of hers persists like an undercurrent motif in her narration. However, the gradual eruption of the hospital leads *Nectar in a Sieve* end not with a note of despair; and optimism thus lurks behind a thin ray of hope for a bright future. And here lies, perhaps, the essence of the novel — acceptance as solution.

REFERENCES

1. Kai Nicholson, *Social Problems in the Indo-Anglian Novel* (Bombay : Jaico, 1972), p. 116.
2. Kamala Markandaya, *Nectar in a Sieve* (New York : New American Library, 1954), pp. 31-32. Hence after the textual insertions are referred with page numbers.
3. S. Cowasjee and V.A. Shahane, *Kamala Markandaya, Modern Indian Fiction*, p. 104.

22

Khushwant Singh's *Delhi* : A Queer Blend of History and Romance

P.K. SINGH

Khushwant's *Delhi* (1990) is a queer blend of history, romance, and sex. The chapters of the novel contain the vivid picturisation of history commencing from Mughal period of Zahiruddin Babar and ending to the assassination of Indira Gandhi. The novel sometimes appears to be a fine travelogue when Khushwant presents the vivid pictures of various roads, lane and historical places of Delhi in its real names, forms and features. The historical events narrated in the different chapters of the novel is seen nicely wrapped with sex and romances. The narrator's, being himself the novelist, sexual encounter with the Bhagmati, a 'hijda' (hermaphrodite), creates a sinister feeling among the readers.

The novel begins with a vivid picturisation of Delhi, alleged to be "misused by rough people they have learnt to conceal their seductive charms under a mask of repulsive ugliness" (p. 1). The citizen of Delhi "spit phlegm and bloody betel-juice everywhere the urge overtakes them; they are loud-mouthed, express familiarity with incestuous abuse and scratch their privates while they talk" (p. 1). Budh Singh, the watchman, of the apartment where hero (narrator) lives, has strong objection about his relation with Bhagmati and so he confides, "everyone is talking about it. They say, take woman, take boy-okay; But a hijda; That is not nice" (p. 6). But the hero remains unaffected by his objections.

Khushwant is keenly aware of the fact that the sexual abuse of minor boys and girls by their near relatives is becoming increasingly common in metropolitan cities and other parts of our country. He states as to how a minister of cabinet has impregnated his daughter-in-law or an Indian Staff of an African Embassy was sexually misused and a college lad writes a letter complaining that his step-mother raped him while his father was out of station. The novelist further shamlessly highlights the sexual abuse of 'hijdas' by different people; some enjoy them like a woman and some others like a boy unnaturally :

> "When men came to expand their lust on 'hijdas' — it is surprising how many prefer them to women — Bhagmati got more patrons than anyone else in her troupe. She could give herself as a woman; she could give herself as a boy. She also discovered that some men preferred to be treated as women. Though limited in her resources, she learnt how to give them pleasure too. There were no variations of sex that Bhagmati found unnatural or did not enjoy. Despite being the plainest of hijdas, she came to be sought by the old young, the potent and impotent, by homosexuals, sadists and mascochists." (p. 30)

The narrator (hero) expresses also his own obnoxious sexual encounter with Bhagmati. He explains, "I felt a desire for sex. I tried to put it out of my mind. Asick, scrutffy hijda — how could.... I was aroused. I pulled her beside me fished out a contraceptive from under my pillow and mouthed her. She directed me inside her. It was no different from a woman's. She smelt of sweet, I avoided her mouth. She pretended to breathe heavily as she were getting worked up. Then sensing my coming to climax she crossed her legs behind my back and began to moan.... She began to play with my nipples — first with her fingers, then with her tongue. She placed her head on my chest and began to stroke my paunch — first with her fingers, then with her tongues. She went on till my reluctance was overcome...with a series of violent heaves she sucked my seed into her in a frenzy of abandon. I lay on top of her-exhausted." (pp. 40-41)

The hero's second sexual encounter happens with the Fraulein Irma Weskermanna, a stenographer working in the West German Embassy. He takes with her a dinner at Moti Mahal and a little of wine with her. When he took initiatives, she begins to put her face forward to receive a kiss on her bony cheeks. Finally, she succeeds in getting her consent for encounter and comes into her bedroom. She picked up her handbag and hurried into the bathroom and came out draped in a dressing-gown. The hero explains thereafter, "Fraulein Weskerman lay on her back and parted her thighs. I entered her without much emotion. She was not a virgin, she was damp but not very excited. All she did was to let out to moan aah and shut her eyes. We lay interlocked without a word or movement neither of us seemed to be getting very much out of it. But neither seemed to have the courage to call it off." (p. 45)

The part four of the novel deals with Musaddi Lal, who belonged to the reign of Sultan Ghiasuddin Balban. His ancestor, he claims proudly, had been scribes in the service of the rulers of Delhi, Raja Anangpal, the Tomar Rajput who built Lal Kot and planted the sacred iron pillars of Vishnu Bhagwan in the middle of the city. They also served Raja Prithvi Raj Chauhan and also Mohammed Ghori. Ram Dulari, the wife of the narrator (Musaddi), was reluctant to have sex with him and whenever he endeavoured, she started to scream. One day Musaddi Lal, however, succeeds to seduce her sulking wife for sex with him. He explains, "under the light of the stars I saw her pale body, the outlines of her rounded breasts and her broad hips. She dried herself with the same Sari and wrapped it round her body. She hesitated, not sure which charpoy to go to. I stretched out my hand to her. She took it and let me pull her beside me. My passion was aroused again. She let me remove her lamp Sari and warm her naked flesh in my embrace. A cry of pain escaped her lips. I knew that I had at long last made Ram Dulari mine. I re-lit the oil lamp and help her wash the stains of blood on the bedsheet. By the time we had finished our bodies were again hungry for each other. So passed the whole night." (p. 61)

In the part five of the novel, Khushwant ironically satirizes the doctors who are often quite negligent to their duties. When the hero goes for an outing with Bhagmati at the tomb of Sultan Feroze Shah Tughlak, he was attacked by the bees violently. His flesh begins to swell, fingers become too fat to be useful and body tingles all over. He drove fast to Ram Manohar Lohia Hospital for emergency treatment of bee stings. There is a cluster of patient around the doctor's table but he is seen engaged in talking on telephone with somebody else. When he speaks in English about complaining to the Health Minister, English works like magic and the doctor starts examining him.

The hero has profound knowledge of History of India. Bhagmati is impressed by his learning. He says as to how Emperor Humayun built a tomb exactly 430 years ago exactly on this day of January 26, 1530. He informs her that the first city of Delhi, called Indraprasth, was built by the Pandavas. He further explains that the Sher Mandal was in fact a library built by Sher Shah Suri. He tells her as to how Humayun's father, Babar, going round his son's sickbed four times prayed to Allah to transfer his son's illness to him and how Humayun had been restored to health and Babar died a few days later. He says that the RED FORT was built by Shah Jahan, who used to sit on the peacock throne therein. He says as to how Aurangzeb killed his brothers and put his father in prison for throne and destroyed Hindu temples.

The novel sometimes appears to be a travelogue as Khushwant gives exact details of almost all the places and roads of Delhi city. He mentions Jama Masjid, Red Fort, Chandni Chowk, Faiz Bazar, Khari Bawli, Connaught Circus and other important places of Delhi in the novel. Interestingly, he mentions history of the places also attached to them.

Khushwant has an excellent knowledge of the phychology of sex. He says that "girls are easy to seduce when they are sixteen than when they are a year or two older. At sixteen they are unsure of themselves and grateful for any reassurance you can give them about their look or brain either will do" (p. 114). He confides her practical experience of seducing a teenager Ms. Georgine, the niece of Carlyle of American Embassy, who had come to Delhi to spend her Christmas vacations. He explains, "any experienced lecher knows that one should not waste words with a teenager because when it comes to real business she gets tongue-tied or can only say 'No'. It is best to talk to her body with your hands. That excites her to a state of speechless acceptance, I ran my fingures up and down her lower arm. She watched them till goose pimples camp up. Thereafter all I had to do was to put my arm around her waist, draw her towards me and mother her lips, eyes, nose, ears and neck with kisses. She moaned helplessly. I slipped my hand under her Kamiz and played with her aaut nipples. Then I undid her pyjama cord and slipped my fingers between her damp thighs. A little gentle ministration with the hand made her convulse and she climaxed groaning "O God; she lay still like a human-sized rubber doll. I put my hand on her bosom. She slapped it and pushed it away. She picked up her cloths and went to the bedroom." (p. 118)

The chapters ten, eleven and twelve gives a historical account of Mughal period of Aurangzeb and Nadir Shah. Shah Jahan became Emperor of Hindustan in October, 1627. He has four sons. Dara Shikoh, Murad, Shuja and Aurangzeb. Aurangzeb was married to Dilras Bano, the daughter of Shah Nawaz Safawi, at the age of seventeen. "The following year Murad, then only fourteen, married Dilras Bano's younger sister and so, besides being our brother, he also became" (p. 147) brother-in-law of Aurangzeb. The differences cropped up among the four brothers for the crown when Shah Jahan fell seriously ill. Other members of royal family advised Shuja and Murad not to behave like the descendants of Mughal dynasty and foundation of which was laid down by Zahiruddin Babar in 1526 and his two sons Humayun and Kamran. Humayun took the light out of the eyes of his brother Kamran and sent him off to Mecca to die in order to grab throne. When Akbar succeeded Humayun, he disposed of Kamaran's son. Likewise Emperor Akbar's reign was disturbed by the revolt of his beloved son Salim Jahangir who in his return had to keep his own impatient son Khusrau in confinement. (p. 153)

The chapter sixteen gives description of the period of last emperor Bahadur Shah Zafar. There was a great fighting between the British army and Mughal loyalists. People also supported strongly to the fighters of Mughal fighters at every nook and corner of Delhi, "General Bakht Khan fought back valiantly. He was everywhere, at the Sabzi Mandi in the morning, at Mori Gate in the afternoon, at Kashmiri Gate in the evening. After sunset he came to the palace to report. The enemy forced his way into the city. The citizens fought them every street. Even women and children hurled on the heads of the assailants. Although age has made our bones brittle we mounted our Arab horse Hamdam and went out to encourage our troops. But Allah willed that we would be taught a lesson in humility." (p. 292)

Queen Victoria died in 1901. When the ship bearing King George and Queen Marry docked in Bombay on 2 December 1911, the hero and his father reached Delhi in order to have the darshan of their rulers and explore possibilities of getting building contracts. At the age of seventeen, his father decides to marry him and a girl of fourteen years was chosen from the neighbouring village. When she was eighteen and he was twenty, they borne two sons. The partition of Bengal by Lord Curzon in 1905 had angered Hindus who felt that it was designed to further divide Hindus and Muslims and create a Muslim state in East Bengal. Young Bengali Hindus and Maharashtrian and some Sikhs vowed to undo the partition and destroy the British rule. In Bengal bombs were thrown at English officers and some were murdered. In Gujarat an attempt was made on the life of Lord Minto who had succeeded Lord Curzon as Viceroy. A Punjabi boy studying in London shot and killed Wylic. These incidents compelled Britishers to withdraw their decision of partition of Bengal. Meanwhile their decision to transfer Capital from Calcutta to Delhi was widely welcomed and the only exceptions were the some Europeans with their business in Calcutta.

Lord Chelmsford was succeeded by a sixty years old Viceroy; arrived in India in 1921 there were agitations among Sikhs to liberate their gurudwaras from hereditary priests. Mahatma Gandhi and his fellow Congressmen were demanding self-rule in the country. Muslims Moplahs of Malabar were agitating against Hindu money lenders. Lord Reading diplomatically first invited Gandhi over a cup of tea and a few months thereafter jailed him and other Congress leaders namely Motilal Nehru and his son Jawaharlal. These leaders have given a call to boycott the visit of the Prince of Wales. Army was send to crush the agitation of Muslim moplahs at Malabar. Lord Reading befriended Indian politicians to know their mind and what kind of men they are. He, however could not suppress the rising tide of Congress. The Congress party swept the polls in 1923 elections and Motilal Nehru became its main spokesman in the Central Assembly. On 23rd March, 1931 Bhagat Singh, Sukh Dev and Rajguru were hanged for committing the murder of an Anglo-Indian sergeant.

The Chapter twenty presents painful pictures of partition of India. Majority of the population of Hadali were Mussalmans and rests were Hindus. Hindus and Sikhs were tradesmen and money-lenders. They lent money to the Mussalmans and when they did not return their money with the interest they were made to pay off by serving them. They used to buy rock salt from the Range and had these fellow take it on their camels to distant cities like Lahore, Amritsar, Ludhiana and Jalandhar. They sold the salt and bought back tea, sugar, spices and silks to sell in their desert villages. Hindus and Sikhs lived in a brick built houses and buffaloes in their courtyards. The Mussalmans lived in Mudhuts and looked after their cattle in exchange for a pot of milk.

Some rumours in the last week of August 1917 of killing Hindus and Sikhs in Rawalpindi and Lahore caused tension in the village. It was heard that Hindus and Sikhs were fleeing eastwards where were not many Mussalmans. Then it was heard that the Mussalmans had got a country of their own called Pakistan and Hadali was in Pakistan. Some elders suggested them to leave Hadali and join other Hindus and Sikhs who were going to Hindustan. But they were reluctant to do so because money were on lent among Mussalmans were yet unrecovered. One day Lachmi, the sister of Ram Rakha was abducted by young Mussalmans and forcibly converted and married to Mussalman young boy. This incident compelled them to leave Hadali. The narrator (Ram Rakha) explains the painful and piquent situation, "We travelled all night and day with hot sand blowing in our faces. We came to Sargodha and found the encampment where thousands of Hindus and Sikhs were waiting to go to India. Our buffaloes were taken away. For many days we lived on stale bread and pickles. Then soldiers came and put us in their trucks. They drove us to Lahore. We passed long lines of people on foot and in bullock card. Those going our way were Sikhs and Hindus. Those coming from the opposite direction were Mussalmans. We saw many Sikhs lying dead on the road with their long hair scattered about and their bearded face covered with flies. We crossed Indo-Pakistan border. There were many more corpses along the road. From the shape of their penises I could tell they were Musslamans. There were lots of women and children among the dead." (p. 325)

The last Chapter of the novel gives a vivid and truthful description of killing of Bhindrawala and Prime Minister Indira Gandhi and the erruption of riot caused by the later's assassination in Delhi in 1984. The narrator explains, "The mob is composed of about fifty young boys armed with iron rods. Some have canisters of petrol in their hands. They surrounded the gurudwara and storm in. They drag out the Bhai and beat him up with their fists and rods." (p. 388)

He further explains as to how Budh Singh was killed by the rioters in heartless manner, "The young gangesters play a cat and mouse game with him. They take turns prodding Budh Singh in the back with their rods. The old fellow is getting tired. He can't fight so many men. As he pauses for breath, an iron rod crashes on his shoulder and brings him down. His Kirpan falls out of his hand. One fellow picks it up and pokes in his bottom. Two lad pounced on him and his arms behind his back. One takes out a pair of scissors and begins to clip off Budh Singh's beard. Budh Singh spits in his face. The fellow slaps him on the face, catches him by his long hair and cuts off a hunk. They've and their fun. They got down to serious business. A boy gets a car tyre, fills its inside rim with petrol and lights. It is a fiery garland. Two boys hold it over Budh Singh and slowly bring it down over his head to his shoulders. Budh Singh screams in agony as he comes down to the ground. The boys laugh and give him the Sikh call of victory; Boley so Nihal : Sat Sri Akal". (p. 391)

Thus, the novel ends giving heart rendering description of Delhi's 1984 riot killing hundreds and wounding thousands innocent Sikhs. The novel has its peculiar style of its own in which Khushwant presents history of India wrapped up in romance and sex.

REFERENCES

1. R.K. Dhawan, "*Three Contemporary Novelists* (Classical Publishing Company, New Delhi, 1985).
2. V.A. Shahane : *Khushwant Singh*, Twayne Publishers, New York, 1972).

23

Submissive Soul : A Study in Salman Rushdie's *Midnight's Children*

RAMESH KUMAR GUPTA

> "The situation of woman is that — she a free and autonomous being like all creatures — nevertheless finds herself living in a world where men compel living in a world where men compel her to assume the status of the other."
>
> (Simone de Beauvoir : *The Second Sex*)

Kate Millett in *Sexual Politics* considers it the 'Powernexus'. Referring Henry Miller's "Sexus" she writes "a male assertion of dominance over a weak, compliant, and rather unintelligent female. It is a case of sexual politics at the fundamental level of copulation.[1] In *Lawerence : Men and Women* Sheila Mcleod also illustrates this term "power-nexus" :

> "Women's work has long been downgraded and devalued when compared to man's work, male muscular strength has been prized above the female capacity for physical endurance, men have been the owners of wealth and property, the wielders of authority, the holders of power, the achievers, the doers, the go-getters, while women have been barred from such apparently desirable positions or behaviour."[2]

In Rushdie's *Midnight's Children* Padma is the partner — partner not only for bed but for life too, a devoted nurse and above all a submissive soul of Saleem Sinai. Padma is a prey of masculine might. She is portrayed only in descriptive manner by Saleem. There are other characters also that figure in the novel, have unwholesome affinity among themselves. Rushdie himself assumes it "a book that discusses the relationships between history and private lives.[3] Dieter Reimenschneider also considers *Midnight's Children* "…is essentially concerned with man's quest for his identity."[4] D.W. Atkinson, a reputed observer, illustrates *Midnight's Children* as an autobiographical novel, projecting grandiosely the 'macro-reality' of national concerns as an extension of the 'macro-reality' of self.[5] Critics have discussed several aspects of the novel but there are a few critics who have discussed Padma. Uma Parameswaran remarks that Padma "is many things within the novel, and certainly deserves a full study". In this paper, the attempt is concentrated on Padma though it is felt that the sexist bias operates against nearly all women characters in the novel.

Padma is a prey of male chauvinistic society. She is depicted in the novel through her animal materiality. Saleem Sinai does not hesitate to say her as : Padma — our plump Padma….sulking magnificently (She can't read… Padma : strong, jolly, a consolation for my last days. But definitely a bitch-in-the manger") (*Midnight's Children* : 1982, p. 24). This explanation does not display her a positive image and it is followed by a still forehead. 'Okay, starve starve, who cares two pice? Another louder, conclusive snort…. Thick of waist, somewhat hairy of forearm, she flounces, gesticulates, exists. Poor Padma (*ibidem.*, p. 24). Padma is compared to a bitch, she cajols, snorts; moves her hand up down up and so on. She is illiterate, ignorant and unpleasant as well. Saleem calls her 'plump', 'thick of waist' and 'somewhat hairy forearm'. He again says Padma "really — truly was a witch?" (*ibid.*, p. 381). This indicates Saleem's repugnant attitude towards Padma.

Padma's works present her as a sheer stereotype. She is busy for Saleem. She cooks food for Saleem, prepares his bed, and after all becomes disappointed when she is ignored by him. Her works have no notice and appreciation. Padma's honest devotion, simplicity and submissiveness have no meaning. Here masculine power claims that man knows better. Padma is illiterate so she is far from reading and writing. But writing is Saleem's estate on which basis — time, history and politics are willingly monopolized by him, as to cooking and making bed are not significant. Saleem appears as an order giver whereas Padma a good maintainer. Saleem ever derides her for illiteracy and passivity. He evinces his hegemonic view by saying : "I attempt to educate her" (*ibid.*, p. 38). He states that he is quite aware of the people, politics, society and culture of India. Saleem, like Rushdie, depicts the socio-economic experience which keep Padma as an illiterate. This is the social order which keep the women uneducated here. This social order explicates it as a case of sex-difference which is founded by male power in our Indian society. Only they have divided their roles and rights on the gender-difference. Cooking food, washing clothes, giving birth to children and nourishing them, making beds for husbands and waiting for them, nurses them are all women's trades and the rest are made for men. *De facto*, man has power from the very beginning so he raises his own status to a high level and degrades women's *et al.* After all, tout *le monde* knows that cooking food is no less than opining history or writing autobiography.

The negative aspect of passionate desire is constructed around Padma for Saleem. As we see in the novel, Saleem does not fulfil Padma's carnal craving and any physical demand. Instead of satiating her he claims that Padma is a mere sample of sensual raven. It implies that man is mighty on the sensual project as well. He elevates symbolic reference of Padma's sexual urge in a vulgar way. But after passing a long period Saleem avows that he is no good in bed. Padma has been deceived into adopting that Saleem must be physically fit. It is a turning point for Saleem to see her only as a bitch in ardour of youth. His manly might appears of no worth. Padma's requirements are emotional and psychic but it is refractory of Saleem to imply that she craves but for sex. Voluntarily, Padma demands to be his gamete and it indicates that carnal desire is not the destination of her life. In esse she would be fortunate if Saleem could give some good, loving, caring, touching and sympathetic jiffies to her. But Saleem has no sense of it. This city dweller Saleem has no time for this vulgar rustic girl. Her only defect or crime is that she has immolated herself at the altar of Saleem's love that has trapped her. Therefore, she is in his custody and pines for his love. Padma says :

> "So then I thought, how to go back to this man who will not love me and only does some foolish writery? (Forgive, Saleem baba, but I must tell it truly. And love, to us women, is the greatest thing to all)." (*Ibid.*, p. 193)

Her submissive-soul is moaning out of Saleem's sense, sympathy and love. Her one thing is to be noted that Padma is a Hindu woman and she loves a man who is a sterile Muslim widower. In spite of all rough and tumble situations she decides to marry and stay with him is a clear indication of her devotional love. The novelist presents a statement through Saleem Sinai in support of Padma's pitiable plight *viz.*,

> "Our Padma Bibi, long-suffering tolerant consoling, is beginning to behave exactly like a traditional Indian wife. (And I, with my distances and self-absorption, like a husband?) O late, in spite of my stoic fatalism about the spreading cracks, I have smelled, on Padma's breath, the dream of an alternative (but impossible) future; ignoring the implacable finalities of inner fissures, she has began to exude the bitter-sweet fragrance of hope-for-marriage. My dung-lotus, who remained impervious for so long to the sneer-lipped barbs hurled by our work force of downy-forearmed women; who placed her cohabitation with me outside and above all codes of social propriety, has seemingly succumbed to a desire for legitimacy...in short, although she has not said a word on the subject, she is waiting for me to make an honest woman of her. The perfume of her sad hopefulness permeates her most innocently solicitous remarks...." (*Ibid.*, pp. 384-85).

She appears as though she has sold her whole life for the sake of his love. Saleem opines her an object of use. He needs warmth of affection, care and food and she is supposed to consummate his all requirements. But in retort, Padma is treated as a 'nympho-maniac' by him. Despite, it is perplexing to justify Saleem's heartless, emotionless and surface notions to her : "I don't blame Padma."

Saleem does not neglect Padma's presence. He cannot bear Padma's absences. He wants her and consequently takes her presence for granted, but then being a male he despises to show his urge. This duality presents his inobservance. He degrades her, derides her, exploits her and still expects her to be loyal to him. In this circumstance it is Padma who loves him and is ever ready to digest his constipated careers. Padma says : "This love, mister," Padma is wailing, "It will drive a woman to craziness." (*Ibid*., p. 193)

In this novel Padma is portrayed more of gaps of absences than presences. Her absence depicts critical background of her past, her family structure and her social status. She appears to be depicted only as a footprint to Saleem the narrator, and is displayed to have only a devoid by way of her human concerns. She has no lobery, no existence and no identity. Her identity is denied when Saleem talks history or politics. "Padma began to cry. 'I never said I didn't believe, she wept.' Of course, every man must tell his story in his own true way; but..." (*Ibid*., p. 211). She is discarded at every level of life. Saleem denies her but the readers have sympathy with Padma. Saleem goes three generations back to initiate his anecdote as, "You see, Padma : I have told this story before." (*Ibid*., p. 365) and compels that in place of knowing him, the readers will have to know a lot of loves, but he has no place of Padma to hold an opinion in his life "Grieve for Saleem — who, orphaned and purified, deprived of the hundred daily pin-pricks of family life, which alone could deflate the great ballooning fantasy of history and bring it down to a more manageably human scale, had been pulled up by his roots to be flung unceremoniously across the years, fated to plunge memoryless into an adulthood whose every aspect grew daily more grotesque." (*Ibid*., p. 345). Padma's past, present, parents and pleasure all are lost in Saleem's story which is also opined worth telling.

Padma is depicted as the 'lotus-Goddess' in the novel. When she was small, she had been named after the lotus goddess by her mother, whose most common appellation amongst village folk is "The One Who Possesses Dung" (*Ibid*., p. 24). Perhaps, there is no contrast at all. In this concern the novelist presents Padma, "Who along with the Yaksa genii, who represent the sacred treasure of the earth, and the sacred rivers, Ganga, Yamuna, Saraswati, and the true goddess, is one of the Guardians of life, beguiling and comforting mortal men while they pass through the dreamweb of Maya. Padma, the Lotus calyx, which grew out of Vishnu's navel, and from which Brahma himself was born; Padma the source, the mother of Time!..." (*Ibid.*, pp. 194-95). The characteristics of masculine power need to recompense man's real disgrace and exploitation of woman by doing out to her some supernatural, and bewildering space in which she is adored as a deity. This bewildering space is the notion of her sex. This imaginary space is an indication to legalize her real exploitation continuously. Padma's reference as the lotus goddess has no meaning to her though she may consider it is, in that she is a willing dupe of the sex politics of India. Padma is Saleem's disdained other, utilizable, exploitable and submissive soul. Here she is presented as a mere commodity of sex. She is not only a slavery of Saleem but also a prey of illiteracy. The novelist presents this paradigm not only for Padma but also for the women in general. Robin Morgan proposes that the new feminist moral vision is in many ways analogous to the vision of reality offered by the new physics. She sees feminism as "crucial to the continuation of sentient life on this planet". It is the key to our survivai and transformation. The reason she offers is that women have over the centuries developed an ethic that is appropriate to the world view that is emerging out of the new physics : they see in terms of relationship and in terms of environmental contexts. Moreover, women have been the custodians of human values for centuries. Their primary value is a reverence for life. This ethic must become the governing world ethic."[7]

Padma is considered to male domination and she wishes to convert her name from Padma Mongril to Naseem Sinai. What Saleem expects, Padma does more to him. That is why she is amongst those who are men's women. Rushdie has illustrated Padma as a 'submissive soul' or 'agonised self' who acts according to her master's voice sans knowing it. She is not free to act according to her choice. She is evinced as a pathetic prey in Saleem's house. The readers of this novel do not regard her as an ideal in Indian ethos. Beauvoir set up a *de facto* trap whereby women are constantly faced with the threat of demission, or back-sliding in "being" of aware of the injustice done to her by masculine power but habit makes them a willing detenu in this world of exploitation and injustice. Padma looks like submissive soul who does not have courage to break a long relationship which has become purportless with no sense of companionship or partnership between gamete and gametes.[8]

Thus, Rushdie's *Midnight's Children* has several qualities, but its gender-difference presents submissive soul of the protagonist Padma and it appears despised and incongruous to all who have faith in the similarity of sexes. She is a stereotype and over-duped figure of woman in a male-chauvinistic society. In this figure woman is marginated while man occupies ample right to dominate in the society.

REFERENCES

1. Kate Millett, *Sexual Politics* (1969 rpt. London : Rupert Hart-Davis, 1971), p. 6.
2. Sheila Mcleod, "The Passion to be Masculine", *Lawerence's Men and Women* (1985, rpt., London : Paladin Grafton Books, 1987), p. 18.
3. Malvika, Rajbans Sanghvi, "You Fight to Like Where You Live," *Indian Express Magazine*, March 20, 1983, p. v.
4. Dieter Reimenschneider, "History and Individual in Anita Desai's *Clear Light of Day* and Salman Rushdie's *Midnight's Children*", *World Literature Written in English*, 23 (1984), p. 196.
5. David W. Atkinson, *Abstracts of English Studies*, 27 (September 1984), 2293.
6. Uma Parameswaran, "Salman Rushdie in Indo-English Literature", *Journal of Indian Writing in English*, 12 (July 1984), p. 24.
7. Robin Morgan, *The Anatomy of Freedom : Farminism, Physics and Global Politics* (New York : Doubleday, 1982), pp. 282-83.
8. Helene Lamore Eisenberg, "The Theme of Demission of the Works of Simone de Beauvoir" (Ph.D. Dissertation, University of California, Berkeley, 1978).